It's Another Ace Book from CGP

This book is for 14-16 year olds.

First we stick in all the <u>really important stuff</u>
you need to do well in the SEG Modular Science GCSE.

Then we have a really good stab at making it funny —
so you'll <u>actually use it</u>.

Simple as that.

CGP are just the best

The central aim of Coordination Group Publications is to produce
top quality books that are carefully written, immaculately
presented and marvellously funny — whilst always making sure
they exactly cover the National Curriculum for each subject.

And then we supply them to as many people as we possibly can,
as <u>cheaply</u> as we possibly can.

Buy our books — they're ace

Higher

This book is suitable for both Higher and Foundation Tier candidates.
The material which is required only for Higher Tier is clearly indicated in blue boxes like this.
In addition, the Higher Tier questions in the Revision Summaries are printed in blue.

Higher

Contents

(SEG Syllabus reference)

Published by Coordination Group Publications Ltd.
Add illustrations by :Sandy Gardner, e-mail: illustrations@sandygardner.co.uk

Consultant Editor: Paddy Gannon BSc MA

ISBN 1-84146-911-4

Groovy website: www.cgpbooks.co.uk

Printed by Elanders Hindson, Newcastle upon Tyne.
Clipart sources: CorelDRAW and VECTOR.

0900

Cells and Enzymes

Unique Features of Plant Cells

You need to be able to draw this _typical plant cell_ with all the features that are different from the animal cells. Look back to Module One to see the similarities between plant and animal cells.

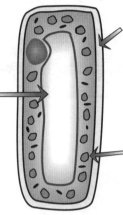

THREE FEATURES THAT ONLY PLANT CELLS HAVE:

1) _RIGID CELL WALL_ made of _cellulose_, gives _support_ for the cell.

2) _VACUOLE_ Contains _cell sap_, a weak solution of sugar and salts, for support and storage.

3) _GREEN CHLOROPLASTS_ containing _chlorophyll_ for _photosynthesis_.

Enzymes

All _enzymes_ work best at a certain temperature. This _optimal_ temperature differs for each type of enzyme. The enzymes within the human body work best at about _37°C_.

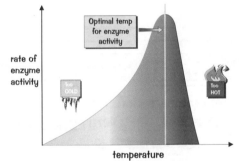

Uses of Enzymes

1) _YEAST_ is used for _MAKING BREAD_ and for _BREWING BEER_, and in both cases the yeast does the business by performing _ANAEROBIC RESPIRATION_. Another word for this process is _FERMENTATION_. Learn this formula for it:

$$\text{Glucose} \rightarrow \text{Alcohol} + \text{Carbon Dioxide} \quad (+ \text{Energy})$$

In bread-making as the yeast gets to work _it's the CO_2 which makes the bread rise_.

In brewing, of course _the alcohol's the most important bit_, but the CO_2 also makes it kinda fizzy.

2) Enzymes are also used in the production of _yoghurt_. _"Lactate"_ bacteria contain the enzymes needed to turn milk into yoghurt. Lactate bacteria are still living in so-called _"live yoghurt"_ and will carry on turning milk into yoghurt if kept at the right temperature. These particular enzymes have an _optimal temperature_ of _48°C_.

Have you learnt it? — let's see, shall we...

Right then, when you're ready, when you think you've learnt it, _cover the page_ and _answer these_:
1) Draw a plant cell and put all the labels on it that make it different from a plant cell.
2) What functions do each of these have?
3) Draw a graph to show how the activity rate of enzymes changes with temperature.
4) Describe three uses of enzymes and write the formula for anaerobic respiration.

Diffusion

Don't be put off by the Fancy Word

"Diffusion" is really simple. It's just the _gradual movement_ of particles from places where there are _lots_ of them to places where there are _less_ of them. That's all it is — _IT'S JUST THE NATURAL TENDENCY FOR STUFF TO SPREAD OUT_.

Unfortunately you also have to _LEARN_ the fancy way of saying the same thing, which is this:

DIFFUSION is the MOVEMENT OF PARTICLES from an area of HIGH CONCENTRATION to an area of LOW CONCENTRATION

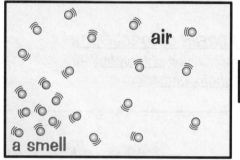 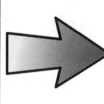 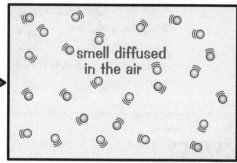

Diffusion Through Cell membranes is kind of Clever...

Cell membranes are kind of clever because they hold everything _inside_ the cell, _BUT_, they let stuff _in and out_ as well. Only very _small molecules_ can diffuse through cell membranes though — things like _sugar_, _water_ or _ions_.

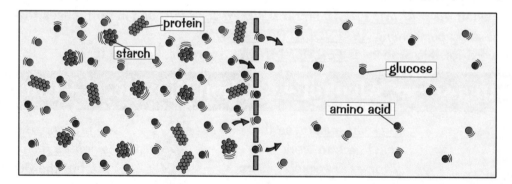

1) Notice that _BIG MOLECULES_ like _STARCH_ or _PROTEINS_ can't diffuse through cell membranes.
2) Just like with diffusion in air, particles flow through the cell membrane from where there's a _HIGH CONCENTRATION_ (a lot of them) to where there's a _LOW CONCENTRATION_ (not such a lot of them).
3) The _RATE OF DIFFUSION_ is directly affected by the concentration gradient — _"The greater the difference in concentration the faster the rate of diffusion"_. Now don't you forget that.

So, how much do you know about diffusion?

Yeah sure it's a pretty book but actually the big idea is to _learn_ all the stuff that's in it.
So learn this page until you can answer these questions _without having to look back_:

1) Write down the fancy definition for diffusion, and then say what it means in your own words.
2) Explain what will and won't diffuse through cell membranes. In which direction do things diffuse?
3) Write down the rule governing the rate of diffusion.

Diffusion

Diffusion of Gases in Plants and Animals

The *simplest type* of diffusion is where *different gases* diffuse through each other, like when a weird smell spreads out through the air in a room. Diffusion of gases happens in both *animals* and *plants*:

Diffusion is an Essential Aspect of Photosynthesis

1) For *PHOTOSYNTHESIS* to happen, *carbon dioxide* gas has to get *inside the leaves*.
2) It does this by *DIFFUSION* through the biddy little holes under the leaf called *stomata*.
3) The CO_2 gas moves to where the concentration is lower, inside the leaf.
4) At the same time *water vapour* and *oxygen* diffuse *out* through the same biddy little holes, to the *lower concentration* outside of the leaf.

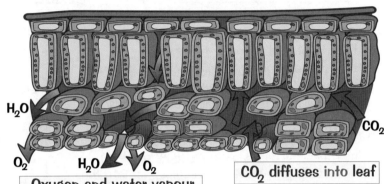

Oxygen and water vapour diffuse out of the leaf

CO_2 diffuses into leaf

Gas Exchange in the Lungs

The *lungs* contain millions and millions of little air sacs called *ALVEOLI* (see diagram opposite) which are specialised to maximise the *diffusion* of oxygen and CO_2. The *ALVEOLI* are an ideal *EXCHANGE SURFACE*. They have:

1) An *ENORMOUS SURFACE AREA* (about 70m² in total).
2) A *MOIST LINING* for dissolving gases.
3) Very *THIN WALLS*.
4) A *COPIOUS BLOOD SUPPLY*.

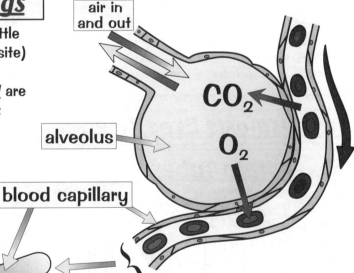

air in and out

alveolus

blood capillary

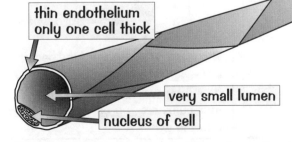

thin endothelium only one cell thick

very small lumen

nucleus of cell

5) The blood capillaries aid the diffusion of gases as their walls are usually *ONLY ONE CELL THICK* making it easy for stuff to pass *in and out* of them.
6) To give you an idea of the size of things here — the capillaries are normally *TOO SMALL* to see.

This is a very easy page to learn...

The big idea is that you should *understand and remember* what goes on and why it all works so well. A clear visual image in your head of these diagrams makes it a lot easier. *Learn* the diagrams, words and all, until you can sketch them out *entirely from memory*.

Osmosis

Osmosis is a Special Case of Diffusion, that's all

OSMOSIS is the _movement of water molecules_ across a _partially permeable membrane_ from a region of **HIGH WATER CONCENTRATION** to a region of **LOW WATER CONCENTRATION**.

1) A _partially permeable membrane_ is just one with _real small holes_ in it. So small, in fact, that _only water molecules_ can pass through them, and bigger molecules like _glucose_ can't.

2) _Visking tubing_ is a partially permeable membrane that you should learn the _name_ of. It's also called _dialysis tubing_ because it's used in _kidney dialysis machines_.

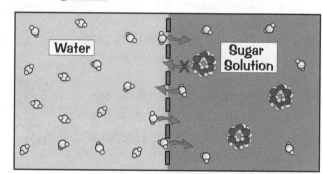

3) The water molecules actually pass _both ways_ through the membrane in a _two-way traffic_.

4) But because there are _more on one side_ than the other there's a steady _net flow_ into the region with _fewer_ water molecules, i.e. into the _stronger solution_ (of glucose).

5) This causes the _glucose-rich_ region to _fill up with water_. The water acts like it's trying to _dilute_ it, so as to _"even up"_ the concentration either side of the membrane.

Net movement of water molecules

6) _OSMOSIS_ makes _plant_ cells _swell up_ if they're surrounded by _weak solution_ and they become **TURGID**. This is real useful for giving _support_ to green plant tissue and for _opening stomatal guard cells_.

7) _Animal_ cells _don't have a cell wall_ and can easily _burst_ if put into pure water because they _take in_ so much water _by osmosis_.

Turgid plant cell   Animal cell bursting

Two Osmosis Experiments — Favourites for the Exams

① Potato Tubes

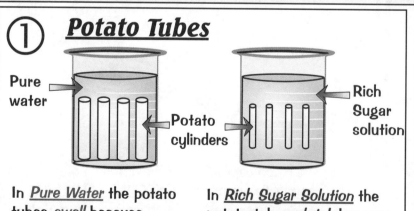

Pure water

Potato cylinders

Rich Sugar solution

In _Pure Water_ the potato tubes _swell_ because water _enters their cells_ by _osmosis_.

In _Rich Sugar Solution_ the potato tubes _shrink_ because water _leaves their cells_ due to _osmosis_.

② Visking Tubing

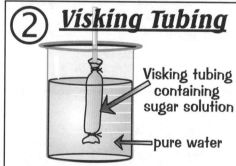

Visking tubing containing sugar solution

pure water

The water _rises up the tube_ because water _enters_ through the Visking tubing by _osmosis_. The _glucose_ molecules are _too big_ to diffuse _out_ into the water.

Learn the facts about osmosis...

Osmosis can be kind of confusing if you don't get to the bottom of it. In normal diffusion, glucose molecules move, but with small enough holes they can't. That's when only water moves through the membrane, and then it's called _osmosis_. Easy peasy, I'd say. _Learn and enjoy._

Active Transport

Active Transport _uses_ Energy to Move Substances

Active transport is the process where cells take up substances _against_ a concentration gradient. This process _requires energy_ and occurs in both _animals_ and _plants_.

Food Digestion

A good example of _active transport_ in animals can be found in the _digestive system_.

1) Food is broken down into _small molecules_ so it can pass from the _small intestine_ into the _bloodstream_.
2) Since the _concentration of molecules_ in the gut is _lower_ than that in the blood, the food molecules _can't simply diffuse_ across the cell membranes.
4) By the rules of diffusion, the food molecules should move in _the other direction_.
5) So the molecules must be _actively transported against_ this concentration gradient.
6) This process _uses energy_ produced by respiration.

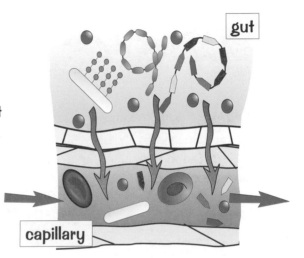

gut

capillary

Root Hair Cell

Active transport is also essential for _transporting substances in plants_.

1) The cells on plant roots grow into long _"hairs"_ which stick out into the soil.
2) This gives the plant a _big surface area_ for absorbing _water and minerals_ from the soil.
3) The concentration of minerals is _higher_ in the _root hair_ cell than in the _soil_ around it.

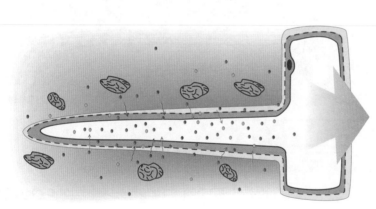

4) So normal diffusion _doesn't_ explain how minerals are _taken up_ into the root hair cell.
5) They should go _the other way_ if they followed the rules of _diffusion_.
6) _Active transport_ allows the plant to absorb minerals _against the concentration gradient_. This is essential for its growth.
7) Active transport _needs energy_ from the plant to make it work. Like in animals, this energy is provided by _respiration_.

Moving house? — call Active Transport...

Well if you're a molecule wanting to move to a new cell you can. But seriously folks, this stuff is easy, just make sure you've understood enough to answer these questions:
1) Why is active transport necessary?
2) Sketch a diagram showing active transport of food molecules in digestion. Include labels showing the differences in concentration between where the food starts and where it ends up.
3) Now do the same showing the uptake of mineral salts into plants.

The Breathing System

The Thorax

Learn this diagram real good.

1) The *THORAX* is the top part of your "body".

2) The *LUNGS* are like *BIG PINK SPONGES*.

3) The *TRACHEA* splits into two tubes called *"BRONCHI"* (each one is "a bronchus"), one going to each lung.

4) The bronchi split into progressively smaller tubes called *BRONCHIOLES*.

5) The bronchioles finally end at small bags called *ALVEOLI* where the gas exchange takes place.

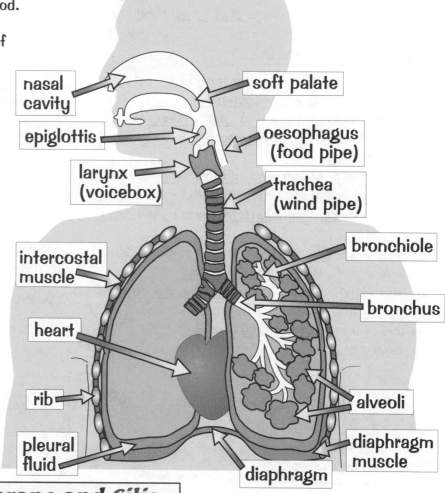

nasal cavity — soft palate
epiglottis — oesophagus (food pipe)
larynx (voicebox) — trachea (wind pipe)
intercostal muscle — bronchiole
heart — bronchus
rib — alveoli
pleural fluid — diaphragm muscle
diaphragm

The Mucous Membrane and Cilia

1) A *mucous membrane* and many *cilia* cover the inside surfaces of the air passages.

2) The membrane produces a sticky liquid called *mucous* which helps to keep conditions *moist and warm* inside the lungs.

3) Mucous also *traps dust particles and bacteria* which might be breathed in.

4) *Cilia are tiny hairs* which constantly wave backwards and forwards, *pushing the mucous* up the trachea.

5) The *mucous entrapped particles* are pushed up *into the larynx* by the cilia, and then *into the oesophagus* to be swallowed.

6) The action of the mucous membrane and cilia helps keep the lungs *clean and free of small particles*.

Stop huffing and puffing and just LEARN IT...

When you practise repeating diagrams from memory, you don't have to draw them really neatly, just sketch them clear enough to label all the important bits. They would never ask you to draw a really fancy diagram in the Exam, but they will expect you to label one. But the only way to be sure you really know a diagram is to sketch it and label it, *all from memory*. Also make sure you learn all the points about the action of mucous and cilia in keeping the lungs clean.

Ventilation and Gas Exchange

Ventilation is...

Breathing In...

1) *Intercostals* and *diaphragm CONTRACT*.
2) *Thorax volume INCREASES*.
3) Air is *DRAWN IN*.

...and Breathing Out

1) *Intercostals* and *diaphragm RELAX*.
2) *Thorax volume DECREASES*.
3) Air is *FORCED OUT*.

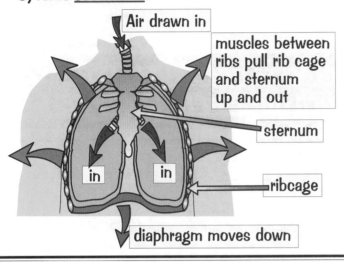

Air drawn in

muscles between ribs pull rib cage and sternum up and out

sternum

in | in

ribcage

diaphragm moves down

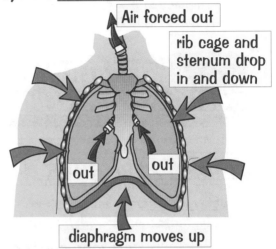

Air forced out

rib cage and sternum drop in and down

out | out

diaphragm moves up

Gaseous Exchange Occurs in the Alveoli

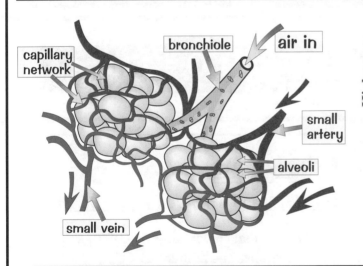

capillary network

bronchiole

air in

small artery

alveoli

small vein

Higher

The *ALVEOLI* are an ideal *EXCHANGE SURFACE*. They have:
1) An *ENORMOUS SURFACE AREA* (about 70m^2 in total).
2) A *MOIST LINING* for dissolving gases.
3) Very *THIN WALLS*.
4) A *COPIOUS BLOOD SUPPLY*.

Higher

1) The job of the lungs is to *transfer OXYGEN to the blood* and to *remove waste CARBON DIOXIDE* from it.

2) To do this *the lungs contain millions of ALVEOLI* where *GAS EXCHANGE* takes place.

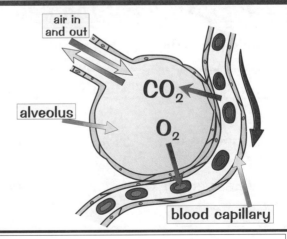

air in and out

alveolus

CO_2

O_2

blood capillary

This is a very easy page to learn...

Notice that the numbered points repeat information that the diagrams already show very clearly. The big idea is that you should *understand and remember* what goes on and why it all works so well. A clear visual image in your head of these diagrams makes it a lot easier.
Learn the diagrams, words and all, until you can sketch them out *entirely from memory*.

Respiration

Respiration is NOT "breathing in and out"

1) Respiration is NOT breathing in and breathing out, as you might think.

2) _Respiration_ actually goes on _in every cell in your body_.

3) _Respiration_ is the process of _converting glucose to energy_.

4) It takes place in _plants_ too. All living things _"respire"_. They _convert "food" into energy_.

> ### RESPIRATION is the process of CONVERTING GLUCOSE TO ENERGY, which goes on IN EVERY CELL

Aerobic Respiration Needs Plenty of Oxygen

1) _Aerobic respiration_ is what happens if there's _plenty of oxygen available_.

2) _"Aerobic"_ just means _"with air"_ and it's _the ideal way to convert glucose into energy_.

You need to learn _THE WORD EQUATION_:

> ### Glucose + Oxygen → Carbon Dioxide + Water + Energy

...and _THE CHEMICAL EQUATION_:

$$C_6H_{12}O_6 + 6O_2 \rightarrow 6CO_2 + 6H_2O + Energy$$

Aerobic respiration takes place in the _mitochondria_

Higher

Composition of Inhaled and Exhaled Air

This is the difference between what you _BREATHE IN_ and what you _BREATHE OUT_:

GAS:	AIR IN:	AIR OUT:
Nitrogen	78%	78%
Oxygen	21%	16%
CO_2	0.03%	4%
Water vapour	Varies	Loads

1) Note that the amount of _OXYGEN USED_ matches the amount of _CO_2 PRODUCED_, as in the above equation.

2) Notice that even with millions of alveoli, you still only absorb _A SMALL PROPORTION OF THE OXYGEN_ in each breath.

One big deep breath and LEARN IT...

The first two sections on this page are the most important and learning them well enough to _scribble them down_ from _memory_ isn't so difficult. Try to visualise the basic page layout and remember how many numbered points there are for each bit. You don't have to write it out word for word, just make sure you remember the important points about each bit.

Anaerobic Respiration

Anaerobic Respiration doesn't use Oxygen at all

1) _Anaerobic respiration_ is what happens if there's _no oxygen available_.

2) "_Anaerobic_" just means "_without_ air" and it's _NOT the best way to convert glucose into energy_.

You need to learn _THE WORD EQUATION_:

$$\text{Glucose} \rightarrow \text{Energy} + \text{Lactic Acid}$$

3) _Anaerobic respiration_ does _not produce nearly as much energy_ as aerobic respiration — but it's useful in emergencies.

Fitness and the Oxygen Debt

1) When you do _vigorous exercise_ and your _body can't supply enough oxygen_ to your muscles they start doing _anaerobic respiration_ instead.

2) _This isn't great_ because _lactic acid builds up_ in the muscles, which gets _painful_.

3) The advantage is that _at least you can keep on using your muscles_ for a while longer.

4) After resorting to anaerobic respiration, when you stop you'll have an _oxygen debt_.

5) In other words _you have to "repay" the oxygen_ which you didn't manage to get to your muscles in time, because _your lungs, heart and blood couldn't keep up with the demand earlier on_.

6) This means you have to _keep breathing hard for a while after you stop_ to get oxygen into your muscles to convert the painful lactic acid to harmless CO_2 and water.

7) When _high levels of CO_2 and lactic acid_ are detected in the blood (by the brain), the _pulse and breathing rate are both increased automatically_ to try and rectify the situation.

8) _A good measure of fitness_ is _how quickly you can recover_ to normal breathing and pulse after doing some vigorous exercise. This is called your _recovery time_.

Anaerobic vs Aerobic Respiration

As long as you have enough _glucose_, _oxygen_ and water, _aerobic_ respiration will allow you to run marathons.

Anaerobic respiration won't allow you to run marathons, but is useful for _short bursts_ of energy.

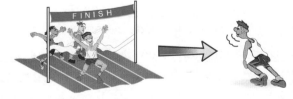

You can't use anaerobic respiration for long before you have to rest to get rid of the _lactic acid_.

Let's see what you know then...

Read the page then see what you can _scribble down_ about each of the three sections. _Then try again_. You don't want to try and learn those eight points about "Oxygen Debt" too formally. It's much better to write your own mini-essay on it and then see what stuff you missed. Enjoy.

The Heart

The heart is made almost entirely of _muscle_. And it's a _double pump_.
Visualise this diagram with its _bigger left side_ full of _red, oxygenated blood_, and its _smaller right side_ full of _blue, deoxygenated blood_.

Learn This Diagram of the Heart with All Its Labels

Right Side

Left Side

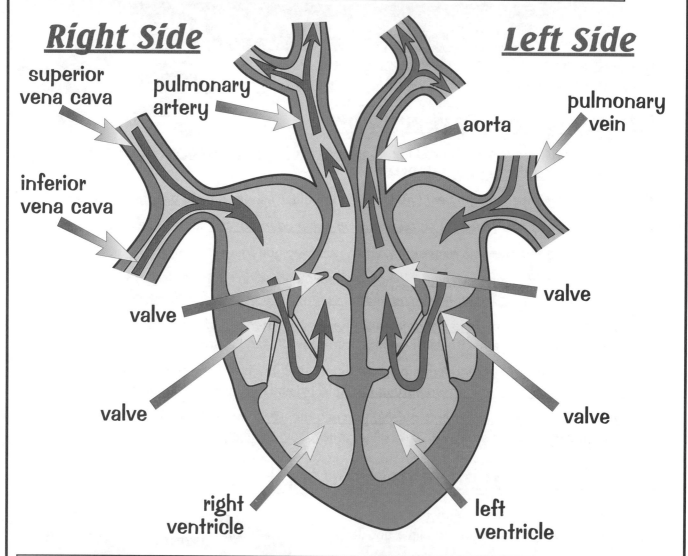

superior vena cava

pulmonary artery

aorta

pulmonary vein

inferior vena cava

valve

valve

valve

valve

right ventricle

left ventricle

Four Extra Details to Delight and Thrill You

1) The _right side_ of the heart receives _deoxygenated blood_ from the body and _pumps it only to the lungs_, so it has _thinner walls_ than the left side because only a _low pressure_ is needed.

2) The _left side_ receives _oxygenated blood_ from the lungs and _pumps it out round the whole body_, so it has _thicker, more muscular walls_ to pump the blood at _high pressure_.

3) The _ventricles_ have thick muscular walls because they need to push blood _round the body_.

4) The _valves_ are for _preventing backflow_ of blood.

OK, let's get to the heart of the matter...

It's important to learn all the labels on the diagram and the direction that the blood is pumped.
There's only one way to be sure you can label it all and that's to learn the diagram until you can sketch it out, with all the labels, _from memory_. Also _learn_ the four points at the bottom.

Blood Vessels

There are three different types of blood vessel and you need to know all about them:

Arteries Carry Blood Under Pressure

1) _ARTERIES_ carry oxygenated blood _away from the heart_.
2) It comes out of the heart at _HIGH PRESSURE_, so the artery walls have to be _STRONG AND ELASTIC_.
3) Note how _THICK_ the walls are compared to the size of the hole down the middle (the "lumen" — silly name!)
4) You can feel your _pulse_ at places where _arteries_ are close to the surface of the body. The pulse is a _measure of heart rate_ as it occurs each time the heart _pumps blood_ into the arteries.

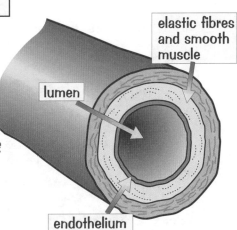

elastic fibres and smooth muscle

lumen

endothelium

Capillaries are Real Small

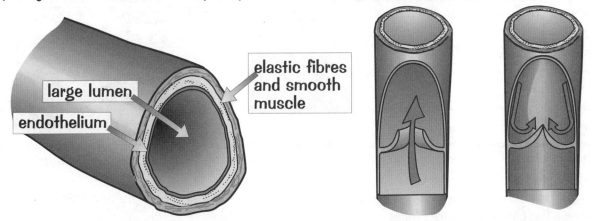

thin endothelium only one cell thick

very small lumen

nucleus of cell

1) Capillaries _deliver food and oxygen_ direct to the body tissues and _take waste products away_.
2) Their walls are usually _ONLY ONE CELL THICK_ to make it easy for stuff _to pass in and out of them_.
3) They are _TOO SMALL_ to see.

Veins Take Blood Back to the Heart

1) _VEINS_ carry _DEOXYGENATED BLOOD_ back to the heart.
2) The blood is at _LOWER PRESSURE_ in the veins so _the walls do not need to be so thick_.
3) They have a _BIGGER LUMEN_ than arteries _TO HELP BLOOD FLOW_.
4) They also have _VALVES_ to help keep the blood flowing _IN THE RIGHT DIRECTION_.

large lumen

endothelium

elastic fibres and smooth muscle

Don't struggle in vain...

Let's face it these are mighty easy diagrams to learn. Just make sure you learn the numbered points as well. I reckon it can't take more than two or three attempts before you can scribble out the whole of this page, diagrams and all, _entirely from memory_. _Concentrate on learning the bits you forgot each time_, of course. Try it and see how right I am!

Leaf Structure

Leaves are Designed for One Thing Only...

— Making Food by Photosynthesis

Make sure you learn these *THREE FEATURES* which help leaves to photosynthesise:

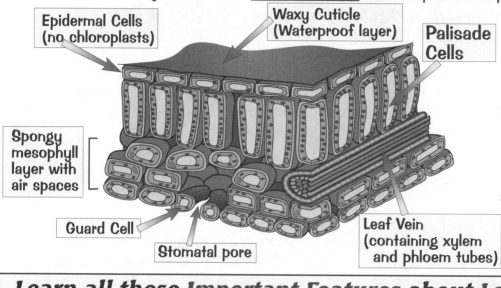

Epidermal Cells (no chloroplasts)

Waxy Cuticle (Waterproof layer)

Palisade Cells

Spongy mesophyll layer with air spaces

Guard Cell

Stomatal pore

Leaf Vein (containing xylem and phloem tubes)

1) Leaves are *thin and flat* to provide a *big surface area* to catch *lots* of sunlight.

2) The *palisade* cells are *near the top* of the leaf and are *packed with chloroplasts*.

3) *Guard cells* control the *movement of gases* into and out of the leaf.

Learn all these Important Features about Leaves

1) The cells in the *palisade layer* are packed with *chloroplasts* which contain lots of *chlorophyll*. This is where the *photosynthesis* goes on.

2) The *palisade* and *spongy layers* are full of *air spaces* to allow CO_2 to reach the palisade cells.

3) The cells in the *epidermis* make *wax* which covers the *leaf surface*, especially the *top surface*. This is to *prevent water loss*.

4) The *lower surface* is full of biddy little holes called *stomata*. They are there to *let CO_2 in*. They also allow water to escape — this is how the *transpiration stream* comes about.

5) *Xylem* and *phloem* vessels cover the whole leaf like tiny *"veins"*, to *deliver water* to every part of the leaf and to *take away the food* (starch) produced by the leaf.

Stomata are Pores which Open and Close Automatically

1) *Stomata* are tiny pores in the leaf which *open and close*.

2) *During photosynthesis* they open to let in *carbon dioxide* and let out *oxygen* and *water*.

3) Two bean-shaped cells called *guard cells* sit at either side of the stomata.

4) They open and close the pore depending on *how much water* they have in them.

Cells *TURGID*, pore *OPENS*

Cells *FLACCID*, pore *CLOSES*

5) When photosynthesis occurs during the day, water moves into the guard cells by *osmosis* and the *pore opens*.

6) *At night* when no photosynthesis can occur, water leaves the guard cells by osmosis and they become flaccid so the *pore closes*.

Higher

Spend some time poring over these facts...

Two spiffing diagrams and a few simple features. What could be easier? Check the clock and give yourself five minutes of intense active learning to see how much you can learn. *"Intense active learning"* means *covering the page* and *scribbling down* the details, but don't take five minutes drawing out a neat diagram of a leaf — that's just a waste of precious time.

Photosynthesis

Photosynthesis Produces Glucose from Sunlight

Photosynthesis is the process that *produces "food"* in plants. The "food" it produces is *glucose*. The *following equation* summarises photosynthesis, so *learn it* well!

$$\text{Carbon dioxide} + \text{Water} \xrightarrow[\text{chlorophyll}]{\text{SUNLIGHT}} \text{glucose} + \text{oxygen}$$

$$6CO_2 + 6H_2O \xrightarrow[\text{chlorophyll}]{\text{SUNLIGHT}} C_6H_{12}O_6 + 6O_2$$

Higher

Four Things are Needed for Photosynthesis to Happen:

1) Light
Usually from the *SUN*

2) Chlorophyll
The *green substance* which is found in *chloroplasts* and which makes leaves look *green*.

This is the "magic" stuff that makes it all happen. Chlorophyll *absorbs the energy in sunlight* and uses it to combine CO_2 and *WATER* to produce *GLUCOSE*. Oxygen is simply a by-product.

3) Carbon dioxide
Enters the leaf from the *AIR* around.

4) Water
Comes *FROM THE SOIL*, up the stem and into the leaf.

Photosynthesis Takes Place in the Leaves of Green Plants

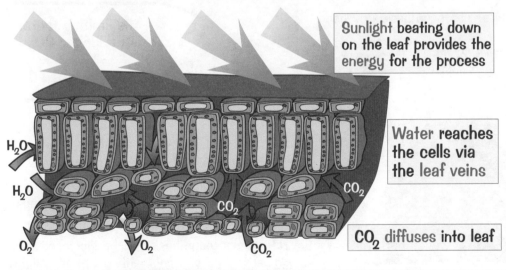

Sunlight beating down on the leaf provides the energy for the process

Water reaches the cells via the leaf veins

CO_2 diffuses into leaf

H_2O H_2O O_2 O_2 CO_2 CO_2 CO_2

1) The *leaves* of plants can get all the things they need for *photosynthesis* from their surroundings.

2) Leaves are *specially designed* for this purpose.

Live and learn...

What you've got to do now is learn everything on this page. Photosynthesis is a "dead cert" for the Exams. On this page you've got a diagram, two points about photosynthesis and the equations, and then the four necessary conditions. Just *keep learning them* until you can *cover the page* and write them all down *from memory*. Only then will you really *know it all*.

The Rate of Photosynthesis

The _RATE_ of _photosynthesis_ is affected by _THREE FACTORS_:

1) THE AMOUNT OF CARBON DIOXIDE AND WATER

_CO_2_ and _water_ are the _raw materials_. Water is never really in short supply in a plant but only _0.03%_ of the air around is CO_2 so it's actually _pretty scarce_ as far as plants are concerned.

2) THE LIGHT INTENSITY

The _chlorophyll_ uses _light energy_ to perform photosynthesis, so the _intensity_ of light is important. The more light there is available the faster photosynthesis can occur.

3) THE WAVELENGTH OF LIGHT

Chlorophyll actually only absorbs the _red_ and _blue_ ends of the _visible light spectrum_, but not the _green light_ in the middle which is _reflected_ back. This is why the plant looks green.

Three Important Graphs for Rate of Photosynthesis

Rate of photosynthesis

Further increase in light intensity doesn't affect the rate

Rate increases with light intensity

light intensity

At any given time one or other of the above _three factors_ will be the _limiting factor_ which is keeping the photosynthesis _down_ at the rate it is.

1) If the _light level_ is raised, the rate of photosynthesis will _increase steadily_ but only up to a _certain point_.

2) Beyond that, it won't make any _difference_ because then it'll be the _CO_2_ level which is wrong and which is now the limiting factor.

3) Conversely, if the _light level_ is too _low_, then changing the amount of CO_2 _won't_ increase the rate of photosynthesis at all — _not until_ the light level is _raised_ to _match_ the CO_2 level .

4) To get _optimum rate_ of photosynthesis you need to make sure that
    1) There's _enough CO_2_
    2) There's _plenty of light_.

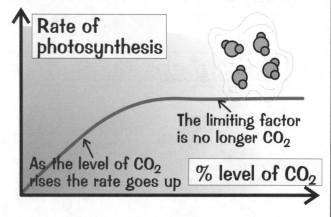

Rate of photosynthesis

The limiting factor is no longer CO_2

As the level of CO_2 rises the rate goes up

% level of CO_2

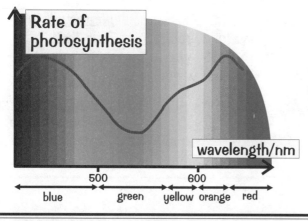

Rate of photosynthesis

wavelength/nm

500   600

blue   green   yellow orange red

5) The _wavelength of light_ is important for photosynthesis as well.

6) Since _red_ and _blue_ light is absorbed the most, the rate of photosynthesis is _greatest_ at those ends of the visible light spectrum.

7) The rate of photosynthesis can be increased by _supplementing natural light_ with red or blue light.

Revision — life isn't all fun and sunshine...

There are three limiting factors, a graph for each and an explanation of the shape of the graphs. _Cover the page_ and practise _recalling all these details_, until you can do it.

How Plants Use the Glucose

For Respiration ①

1) Plants _manufacture glucose_ in their _leaves_.
2) They then use some of the glucose initially for _respiration_ (they also need _oxygen_ for this.)
3) This _releases energy_ which enables them to _convert_ the rest of the glucose into various _other useful substances_ which they can use to _build new cells_ and _grow_.
4) To produce some of these substances they also need to _gather_ a few _minerals_ from the soil.

② Making Fruits

GLUCOSE is turned into _SUCROSE_ for storing in _FRUITS_.
Fruits deliberately _taste nice_ so that animals will eat them and so _spread the seeds_ all over the place.

③ Stored as Starch

Glucose is turned into _starch_ and _stored_ in roots, stems and leaves, ready for use when photosynthesis isn't happening, like in the _winter_.

STARCH is _INSOLUBLE_ which makes it much _better_ for _storing_, because it doesn't bloat the storage cells by _osmosis_ like glucose would.

Potato and carrot plants store a lot of starch in their roots over the winter to enable a new plant to grow from it the following spring. We eat the swollen roots!

④ Stored in Seeds

GLUCOSE is turned into _LIPIDS_ (fats and oils) for storing in _SEEDS_. _Sunflower seeds_, for example, contain a lot of oil — we get _cooking oil_ and _margarine_ from them.

⑤ Making Proteins

GLUCOSE is combined with _NITRATES_ (collected from the _soil)_ to make _AMINO ACIDS_, which are then made into _PROTEINS_.

⑥ Making Cell Walls

GLUCOSE is converted into _CELLULOSE_ for making _cell walls_, especially in a rapidly growing plant.

Higher Higher Higher   *Higher Higher Higher*

"Sugar it", that's what I say...

There are six things that plants do with glucose. Can you spot them? If so, _learn them_, _cover the page_, and then display your new-found knowledge. In other words, sketch out the diagram and _scribble down_ the six ways that plants use glucose, including all the extra details.

Growth Hormones in Plants

Auxins are Plant Growth Hormones

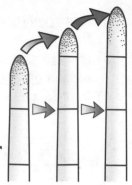

1) _Auxins_ are _hormones_ which _control growth_ at the _tips_ of _shoots_ and _roots_.
2) Auxin is produced in the _tips_ and _diffuses backwards_ to stimulate the _cell elongation process_ which occurs in the cells _just behind_ the tips.
3) If the tip of a shoot is _removed_, no auxin will be available and the shoot _may stop growing_.
4) Shoot tips also produce substances which _inhibit_ the growth of _side shoots_. If the tips are _removed_ it can result in a lot of _side shoots_ because the inhibitor substance is no longer present. Hence, _hedge clipping_ promotes _bushier hedges_, because it produces lots of side shoots.

Commercial Use of Plant Hormones

1) Growing from Cuttings with Rooting Compound

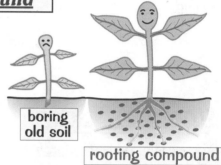

1) A _cutting_ is part of a plant that has been _cut off it_, like the end of a branch with a few leaves on it.
2) Normally, if you stick cuttings in the soil they _won't grow_, but if you add _rooting compound_, which contains a plant _growth hormone_, they will produce roots rapidly and start growing as _new plants_.
3) This enables growers to produce lots of _clones_ (exact copies) of a really good plant _very quickly_.

boring old soil

rooting compound

2) Killing Weeds

1) Most weeds growing in fields of crops or in a lawn are _broad-leaved_, in contrast to grass which has very _narrow leaves_.
2) _Selective weedkillers_ have been developed from plant _growth hormones_ which only affects the broad-leaved plants.
3) It _disrupts_ their normal _growth patterns_, and soon _kills_ them leaving the grass untouched.

Unhappy weeds

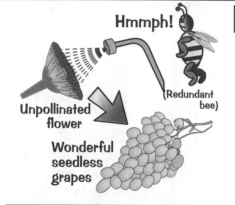

Hmmph!

(Redundant bee)

Unpollinated flower

Wonderful seedless grapes

3) Producing Seedless Fruit

1) Fruits normally only grow on plants which have been _pollinated by insects_, with the inevitable _seeds_ in the middle of the fruit. If the plant _doesn't_ get pollinated, the fruits and seeds _don't grow_.
2) However, if _growth hormones_ are applied to _unpollinated flowers_ the _fruits will grow_ but the _seeds won't_!
3) This is great. Seedless satsumas and seedless grapes are just _so much nicer_ than the "natural" ones full of pips!

Remember, serious learning always bears fruit...

Another blissfully easy page. Just make sure you learn enough about each bit to answer a 3 or 4 mark Exam question on it. As usual the sections are split into numbered points to help you remember them. _So learn them_. Then _cover the page_ and _scribble down_ the points for each. And tell me this — if you can't do it now, what makes you think it'll all suddenly "come back to you" in the Exam?

Water and Mineral Salts

Water Supports Plant Tissues

1) When a plant is _well watered_, all its cells will draw water into themselves and become _turgid_.

2) The contents of the cell start to _push against the cell wall_, kind of like a balloon in a shoebox, and thereby give _support_ to the plant tissues.

Add water

Flaccid Cell   Turgid Cell

3) _Leaves_ are entirely supported by this _turgor pressure_. We know this because if there's no water in the soil, a plant starts to _wilt_, the leaves _droop_ and the plant _dies_. This is because the cells start to _lose water_ and thus lose their turgor pressure.

Water Moves into cells By Osmosis

Turgid Cell

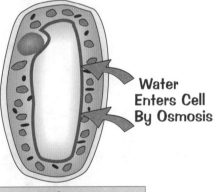

Water Enters Cell By Osmosis

High Water Concentration Outside

Flaccid Cell

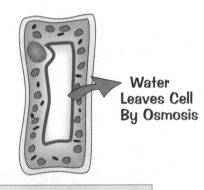

Water Leaves Cell By Osmosis

Low Water Concentration Outside

Plasmolysis

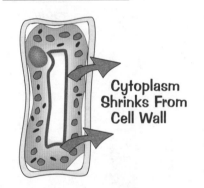

Cytoplasm Shrinks From Cell Wall

Very Low Water Concentration Outside

1) The movement of water into and out of cells happens by _osmosis_.

2) When a plant is well watered there is a _high concentration_ of water surrounding its cells and so water moves into the cells making them _turgid_.

3) A _low water concentration_ outside causes water to leave the cells and they become _flaccid_.

4) _Plasmolysis_ occurs under _very dry_ conditions, when so much water leaves the cell that the _cytoplasm shrinks_ and moves away from the cell wall.

Minerals Are Needed for Healthy Growth

1) For _healthy growth_ plants need _minerals_ which they can only obtain _from the soil_.

2) _Nitrates_ are needed in large amounts for _protein synthesis_.

3) Smaller amounts of _iron_ and _magnesium_ are needed for _making chlorophyll_.

OK, let's see what you know..

When you think you've _**LEARNT**_ everything on this page, _cover it up_ and do these:
1) Why are water and mineral salts important to plants?
2) Sketch a diagram showing a plant cell in _very low_, _low_ and _high_ water concentration conditions.

18

Transport Systems in Plants

18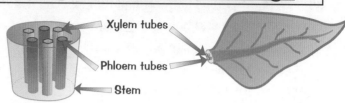

18 *Water, Minerals & Transport in Plants*

Plants need to transport various things around inside themselves. They have tubes for it.

Phloem and Xylem Vessels Transport Different Things

1) Plants have _two separate sets of tubes_ for transporting stuff around the plant.
2) _Both_ sets of tubes go to _every part of the plant_, but they are totally _separate_.
3) They usually run _alongside_ each other.

Xylem tubes
Phloem tubes
Stem

Phloem Tubes transport Food:

1) Made of _living cells_ with _perforated end-plates_ to allow stuff to flow through.
2) They transport _food_ made in the _leaves_ to _all other parts_ of the plant, in _both directions_.
3) They carry _starch_, _fats_, _proteins_ etc. to _growing regions_ in _shoot tips_ and _root tips_ and to/from _storage organs_ in the _roots_.

Water and food

Xylem Tubes take water UP:

1) Made of _dead cells_ joined end to end with _no end walls_ between them.
2) The side walls are _strong and stiff_ and contain _lignin_. This gives the plant _support_.
3) They carry _water and minerals_ from the _roots_ (see below) up to the leaves in the transpiration stream.

Water and minerals

Water and Minerals Enter the Plant Through the Roots

1) Plant roots take up dissolved _mineral salts_ by _diffusion_.

18 **Higher Higher**

2) If the concentration of minerals outside the root is lower than inside, the root takes up mineral ions by _active transport_. (see P. 5)

3) Root cells take up water by _osmosis_.

4) They have a _large surface area_ and very _thin walls_ to help water uptake.

18 **Higher Higher**

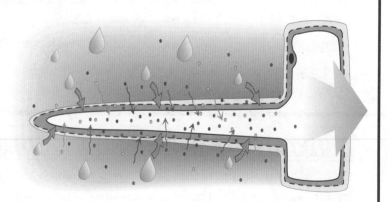

Well that seems to be about the top and bottom of it...

This is an easy page. Learn how substances get around the plant by transport systems. Make sure you know how and where plants get water and mineral salts. Cover the page and scribble it all down with detailed sketches. Then do it again, _until you get it all_.

18
SEG Syllabus   Module Six — Vital Exchanges

The Transpiration Stream

Transpiration is the constant Flow of Water up the Plant

1) It's caused by the _evaporation_ of water from inside _the leaves_.
2) Water evaporates from the plant through the _stomata_.
3) This creates a _slight shortage_ of water in the leaf which _draws more water up_ from the rest of the plant which _in turn_ draws more up from the _roots_.
4) It has _two beneficial effects_: a) _it transports minerals_ from the soil
                                      b) it _cools_ the plant.

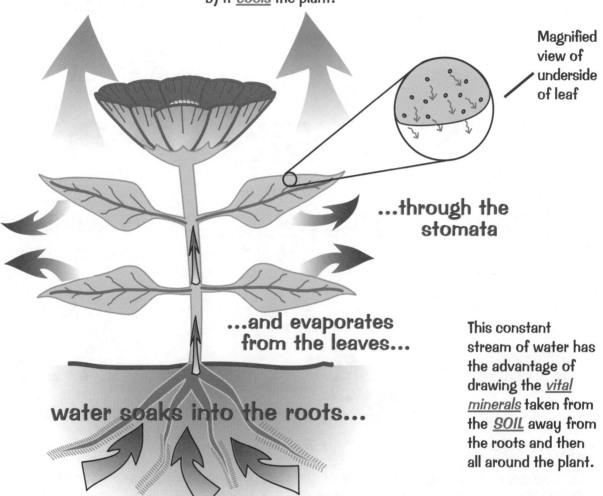

Magnified view of underside of leaf

...through the stomata

...and evaporates from the leaves...

water soaks into the roots...

This constant stream of water has the advantage of drawing the _vital minerals_ taken from the _SOIL_ away from the roots and then all around the plant.

4 Factors which affect it

The _rate of transpiration_ is affected by _four things_:
   1) Amount of _light_
   2) _Temperature_
   3) Amount of _air movement_
   4) _Humidity_ of the surrounding air

It's surely obvious that the _biggest_ rate of transpiration occurs in _hot_, _dry_, _windy_, _sunny_ conditions i.e. perfect clothes-drying weather.

By contrast, a _cool_, _cloudy_, _muggy_, _miserable day_ with _no wind_ will produce _minimum transpiration_.

It helps if you're quick on the uptake...

There's quite a lot of information on this page. You could try learning the numbered points, but you'll find a better plan is to do a _mini-essay_ on transpiration and write down everything you can think of. Then look back to see what you've forgotten. Then do it again! _Till you get it all_.

Food Webs

A Woodland Food Web

Food webs are pretty easy really. Hideously easy in fact.

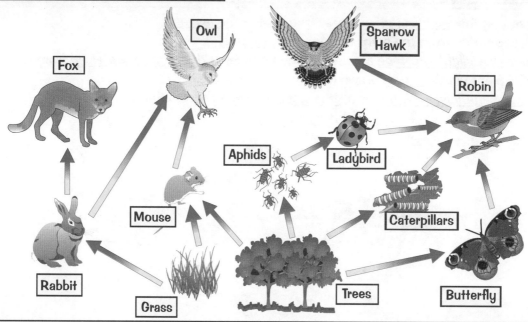

Food Chains — the Arrows show where the Energy goes

1) A *food chain* is just part of a *food web*, starting at the bottom and *following the arrows* up.
2) Remember, the *arrows* show which way the *food energy travels*.
3) Don't mix up *who eats who* either!
   The arrow means *"IS EATEN BY"*, so you *follow the arrow* to the one doing the *eating*.
4) From the woodland food web we could take this *food chain*:

Terminology you need to know

1) *PRODUCER* — all *plants* are *producers*. They use the Sun's energy to produce food energy.
2) *HERBIVORE* — animals which *only eat plants*, e.g. rabbits, caterpillars, aphids.
3) *CONSUMER* — all *animals* are *consumers*. All *plants* are *not*, because they are producers.
4) *PRIMARY CONSUMER* — animal which eats *producers* (plants).
5) *SECONDARY CONSUMER* — animal which eats primary consumers.
6) *TERTIARY CONSUMER* — animal which eats secondary consumers.
7) *CARNIVORE* — eats *only animals*, never plants.
8) *TOP CARNIVORE* — is *not eaten by anything else*, except decomposers after it dies.
9) *OMNIVORE* — eats *both plants and animals*
10) *DECOMPOSER* — lives off all *dead material* — producers, consumers, top carnivore, the lot.
11) *TROPHIC LEVEL* — each *step* along a *food chain* is a trophic level.

Learn about food webs, terminology and all...

That's got to be the prettiest food web ever drawn, wouldn't you say? Yeah well, anyway, the pretty pictures are the easy bit. It's those *11 definitions* which you really need to work at. That's what'll sort out the sheep from the goats in the Exam. So make sure you *know them all*.

The Effects of Pesticides

Pesticides Disturb Food Chains

1) _Pesticides_ are sprayed onto most _crops_ to _kill_ the various _insects_ that can _damage_ the crops.

2) Unfortunately, they _also kill_ lots of _harmless_ insects such as _bees_ and _butterflies_.

3) Destroying these insects is _damaging_ because they are _pollinators_, essential for plant reproduction.

4) Their destruction can also cause _a shortage of food_ for many _insect-eating birds_.

5) _Pesticides_ tend to be _poisonous_ and there's always the danger of the poison _passing on_ to _other animals_ (as well as _humans_) causing food chains to be _disturbed_.

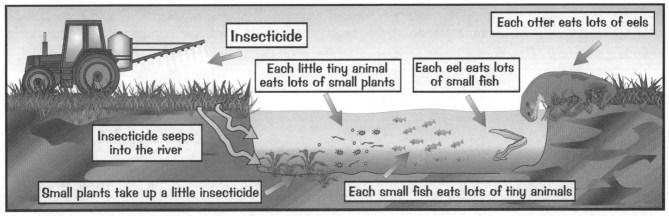

Insecticide

Each otter eats lots of eels

Each little tiny animal eats lots of small plants

Each eel eats lots of small fish

Insecticide seeps into the river

Small plants take up a little insecticide

Each small fish eats lots of tiny animals

1) This is well illustrated by the case of _otters_ which were almost _wiped out_ over much of crop-dominated Southern England by _DDT_ in the early 1960s.

2) The diagram shows the _food chain_ which ends with the _otter_.

3) _DDT_ is _not excreted_ so it _accumulates_ along the _food chain_

4) The _otter_ ends up with _all the DDT_ collected by all the other animals.

Toxin levels Increase along a Food Chain

1) When a toxin like _DDT_ enters a food chain it _increases_ in concentration at each _trophic level_.

2) In the above example a _small_ amount of _DDT_ enters the food chain at the level of the _producers_, small water plants.

3) These plants are then eaten by the _primary consumers_, (the small fish), which take in the poison.

4) At each trophic level in the food chain the level of _DDT_ increases because each consumer eats more _biomass_.

5) By the time you reach the _top carnivore_, the poor old otter, the level of _DDT_ is high enough to cause _death_.

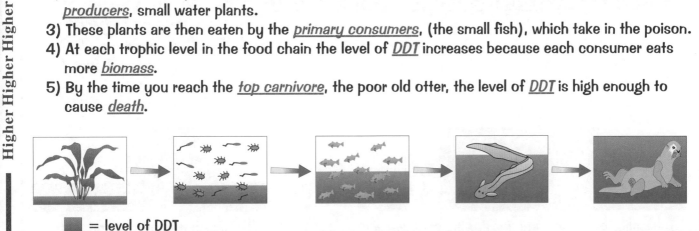

■ = level of DDT

Don't get bugged by revision — just learn and enjoy...

Make sure you know the problems which can arise from using _pesticides_ and how toxins like these can build up in a food chain. You have to learn the details carefully. _Mini-essay_ time again I'd say. _Cover the page and scribble..._

Number & Biomass Pyramids

This is hideously easy too. Just <u>make sure you know</u> what <u>all</u> the pyramids mean.

Each Trophic Level you go up, there's fewer of them...

5000 dandelions...   feed..   <u>100</u> rabbits...   which feed....   <u>one</u> fox.

<u>IN OTHER WORDS</u>, each time you go <u>up one level</u> (one trophic level) the <u>number of organisms goes down</u> — <u>A LOT</u>. It takes <u>a lot</u> of food from the level <u>below</u> to keep any one animal alive. This gives us the good old <u>number pyramid</u>:

<table>
<tr><td colspan="3" align="center">1 Fox</td></tr>
<tr><td colspan="3" align="center">100 Rabbits</td></tr>
<tr><td colspan="3" align="center">5,000 Dandelions</td></tr>
</table>

<u>A typical pyramid of numbers</u>

This is the <u>basic idea</u> anyway. But there are cases where the pyramid is <u>not a pyramid at all</u>:

Number Pyramids Sometimes Look Wrong

This is a <u>pyramid</u> except for the <u>top layer</u> which goes <u>huge</u>:

| 500 Fleas |
| 1 Fox |
| 100 Rabbits |
| 5,000 Dandelions |

This is a <u>pyramid</u> apart from the <u>bottom layer</u> which is <u>way too small</u>:

| 1 Partridge |
| 1000 Ladybirds |
| 3,000 Aphids |
| 1 Pear tree |

Biomass Pyramids Never Look Wrong

When <u>number pyramids</u> seem to go <u>wrong</u> like this, then the good old <u>PYRAMID OF BIOMASS</u> comes to the rescue. <u>Biomass</u> is just how much all the creatures at each level would <u>"weigh"</u> if you <u>put them all together</u>. So the <u>one pear tree</u> would have a <u>big biomass</u> and the <u>hundreds of fleas</u> would have <u>a very small biomass</u>. Biomass pyramids are <u>ALWAYS the right shape</u>:

| Fleas |
| Fox |
| Rabbits |
| Dandelions |

| Partridge |
| Ladybirds |
| Aphids |
| Pear tree |

Basically, <u>biomass pyramids</u> are the only <u>sensible</u> way to do it — it's just that <u>number pyramids</u> are <u>easier to understand</u>.

Now children, get your coloured wooden blocks out...

...hideously easy...

Energy Loss & Efficient Food

All that Energy just Disappears Somehow...

1) Energy from the _SUN_ is the _source of energy_ for _all life on Earth_.

2) _Plants_ convert _a small %_ of the light energy that falls on them _into glucose_.

3) This _energy_ then works its way through the _food web_.

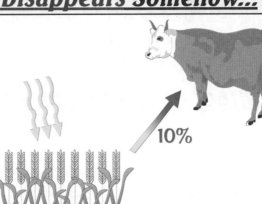

10%

10%

4) But _90%_ is lost at each stage.

5) So _trophic level 2_ (e.g. cows) contains _only 10%_ of the total chemical energy (food energy) which is stored in _trophic level 1_ (e.g. feed).

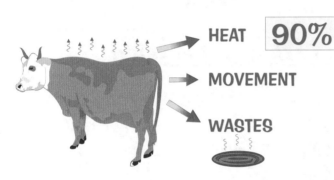

HEAT **90%**

MOVEMENT

WASTES

6) The _90%_ of the _ENERGY lost_ at each stage is used for _staying alive_, i.e. in _respiration_, which powers _all life processes_, including _movement_.

7) Most of this energy is eventually _lost to the surroundings_ as _heat_.

8) _Some energy_ is also lost from the food chain in the _droppings_ — they burn when dried, proving they still have chemical energy in them.

Try it next time you're camping — you'll find you enjoy your midnight sausages that much more when cooked over a blazing mound of dried sheep poo.

"Efficient" Food Production

1) _For a given area of land_, you can produce _a lot more food_ (for humans) by growing _crops_ rather than by _grazing animals_.

2) This is _obvious_. You are _cutting out_ an _extra trophic level_. Remember, only _10%_ of what _beef cattle eat_ becomes _useful meat_ for people to eat.

3) In countries where good agricultural land is _scarce_, they can feed _far more people_ growing _good crops_ than by _grazing cattle or sheep_ for _meat or milk_.

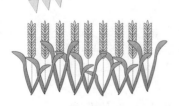

10%

4) However, don't forget that just eating _crops_ can quickly lead to _malnutrition_ through lack of essential _proteins_ and _minerals_, unless a varied enough diet is achieved.

Don't have a cow — just learn it...

It's simple really — energy from the Sun is converted to food energy by plants. Don't forget at each step in the food chain 90% of energy is lost and only 10% gets passed on. You have to learn the details carefully. _Mini-essay_ time again I'd say. _Cover the page and scribble..._

Decomposers & the Carbon Cycle

Energy Flow and Cycles in Ecosystems

1) _Living things_ are made of _materials_ they take from the world around them.

2) When they _decompose_, ashes are returned to ashes, and dust to dust, as it were.

3) In other words _the elements they contain_ are returned to the _soil_ where they came from _originally_.

4) The elements are then _used by plants_ to grow and the whole cycle _repeats_ over and over again.

Bacteria and Fungi are Decomposers

1) _Two organisms_ which break down plant matter and dead animals are _bacteria_ and _fungi_.

2) They work everywhere in _nature_, and also in _compost heaps_ and _sewage works_.

3) All the important _elements_ are thus _recycled_:
   Carbon, _Hydrogen_, _Oxygen_ and _Nitrogen_.

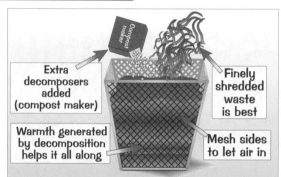

Extra decomposers added (compost maker)

Compost maker

Finely shredded waste is best

Warmth generated by decomposition helps it all along

Mesh sides to let air in

There's a kid I know, and everyone calls him "the party mushroom". I'm not sure why really — they just say he's a fun guy to be with...

The Carbon Cycle Shows how Carbon is Recycled

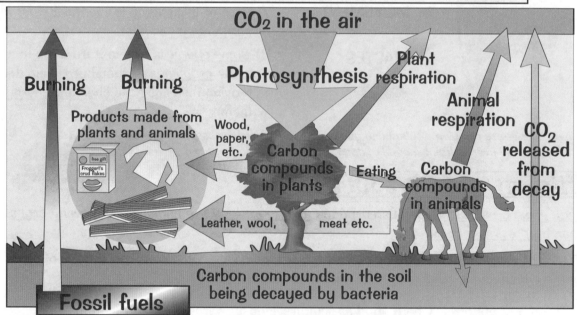

CO_2 in the air

Burning   Burning

Photosynthesis   Plant respiration

Animal respiration

CO_2 released from decay

Products made from plants and animals

Wood, paper, etc.

Carbon compounds in plants

Eating

Carbon compounds in animals

Froggatt's crud flakes   free gift

Leather, wool,   meat etc.

Fossil fuels

Carbon compounds in the soil being decayed by bacteria

This diagram isn't half as bad as it looks. _LEARN_ these important points:

1) There's only _one arrow_ going _DOWN_. The whole thing is "powered" by _photosynthesis_.

2) Both plant and animal _respiration_ puts CO_2 _back into the atmosphere_.

3) _Plants_ convert the carbon in CO_2 _from the air_ into _fats_, _carbohydrates_ and _proteins_.

4) These can then go _three ways_: _be eaten_, _decay_ or be turned into _useful products_ by man.

5) _Eating_ transfers some of the fats, proteins and carbohydrates to _new_ fats, carbohydrates and proteins _in the animal_ doing the eating.

6) Ultimately these plant and animal products either _decay_ or are _burned_ and CO_2 _is released_.

On Ilkley Moor ba 'tat, On Ilkley Moor ba 'tat...

...where the dogs play football.

Learn what decomposers do and the two organisms mentioned. They like asking about that. There's another version of the carbon cycle in Module Nine which you really should look at, but this one is easier to understand. Practise _scribbling_ it out _from memory_. And _keep trying till you can_.

The Nitrogen Cycle

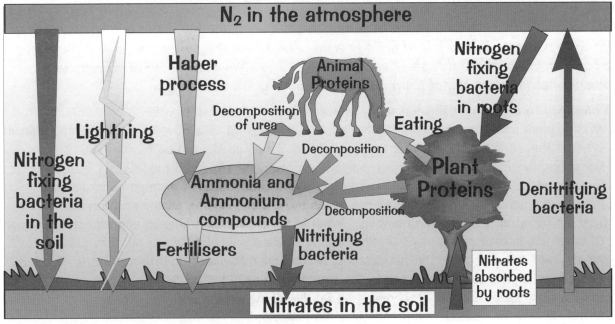

N$_2$ in the atmosphere — Haber process — Lightning — Nitrogen fixing bacteria in the soil — Fertilisers — Ammonia and Ammonium compounds — Nitrifying bacteria — Decomposition of urea — Decomposition — Animal Proteins — Eating — Decomposition — Plant Proteins — Nitrogen fixing bacteria in roots — Denitrifying bacteria — Nitrates absorbed by roots — Nitrates in the soil

1) The _atmosphere_ contains _78% nitrogen gas_, N$_2$.

2) This is _very unreactive_ and cannot be used _directly_ by plants or animals.

3) _Nitrogen_ is an _important element_ in making _protein_ and also _DNA_, so we really need it.

4) Nitrogen in the air has to be turned into _nitrates_, NO$_3^-$, or _ammonium ions_, NH$_4^+$, before plants can use it. _Animals_ can only use _proteins_ made by plants.

6) _Nitrogen fixation_ is the process of turning _N$_2$ from the air_ into a _more reactive form_ which _plants can use_ (and no it isn't an obsession with breathing in and out).

7) There are _THREE MAIN WAYS_ that it happens: 1) _Lightning_,   2) _Nitrogen fixing bacteria_ in roots and soil,   3) _The manufacture of artificial fertilisers_ by the _Haber process_.

8) There are _four_ different types of _bacteria_ involved in the nitrogen cycle:

   a) _NITRIFYING BACTERIA_ — these turn _ammonium compounds_ in decaying matter into _useful nitrates_

   b) _NITROGEN-FIXING BACTERIA_ — these turn useless _atmospheric N$_2$_ into useful _nitrates_.

   c) _PUTREFYING BACTERIA_ (decomposers) — these decompose _proteins_ and _urea_ into _ammonia_ or _ammonium compounds_.

   d) _DE-NITRIFYING BACTERIA_ — these turn _nitrates_ back into _N$_2$ gas_. This is of no benefit.

9) Some _nitrogen-fixing bacteria_ live in the _soil_. Others live a _mutualistic relationship_ with certain plants, called _legumes_, by living in _nodules_ in their _roots_ — the bacteria get _food_ from the plant, and the plant gets _nitrogen compounds_ from the bacteria — to make into _proteins_.

10) _Any organic waste_, e.g. rotting plants or dead animals or animal poo, will contain _useful nitrogen compounds_ (proteins), so they all make _good fertiliser_ if they're put back into the _soil_.

11) _Leguminous plants_ (legumes) such as _clover_ are useful in _crop rotation schemes_, where the field is _left for a year_ to just grow _clover_, and then it's all simply _ploughed back into the soil_. This adds a lot of _nitrates_ to the soil when the plants _decay_.

12) _Lightning_ adds nitrates to the soil by _splitting up N$_2$_ into nitrogen _atoms_ which react with the _oxygen_ in the air to form _oxides of nitrogen_. These then _dissolve in rain_, and fall to the ground where they combine with other things to form _nitrates_.

By gum, you young 'uns have some stuff to learn...

It's really "grisly grimsdike" is the Nitrogen Cycle, I think. But the fun guys at the Exam Boards want you to know all about it, so there you go. _Have a good time... and smile!_

Revision Summary for Module Six

Phew, there's a lot of stuff to learn in Module Six. From all that grisly "open heart surgery" type stuff, to dead otters. Mind you, it's all fairly straightforward and factual — you know, nothing difficult to understand, just lots of facts to learn. And lots of gory diagrams. You know the big plan with these questions though. Keep practising till you can whizz them all off without a moment's hesitation on any of them. It's a nice trick if you can do it.

1) Compared to an animal cell what extra features does a plant cell have?
2) Why do plant cells have vacuoles? What adaptation do plant cells have to allow photosynthesis?
3) What is the word equation for fermentation? What two products use fermentation?
4) Name another food product that is made using enzymes. How is it made?
5) Give the strict definition of diffusion. Sketch how a smell diffuses through air in a room.
6) Draw a diagram showing which way the gases move between the alveoli and the blood.
7) Give the full strict definition of osmosis. What is the difference between osmosis and diffusion?
8) Of what use is osmosis to plants? What happens when animal cells are put into pure water?
9) What is active transport? List two ways in which active transport is different from diffusion.
10) Why is active transport necessary in the digestion of food molecules?
11) Draw a diagram of the thorax, showing all the breathing equipment.
12) What role do the mucous membrane and the cilia play?
13) Describe what happens during breathing in and breathing out. Be sure to give all the details.
14) Where are alveoli found? How big are they and what are they for? Give four features.
15) Give the definition for respiration. What is "aerobic respiration"? Give word and symbol equations.
16) What is "anaerobic respiration"? Give the word equation for what happens in our bodies.
17) Explain about fitness and the oxygen debt.
18) Sketch the diagram of the heart with all its labels.
19) Sketch a heart, an artery, a capillary, and a vein, with labels. Explain the features of all four.
20) Sketch the cross-section of a leaf with seven labels. What is the leaf for?
21) Explain what stomata do and how they do it. How is osmosis involved in the action of stomata?
22) Write down the word equation for photosynthesis. Write down the symbol equation.
23) Sketch a leaf and show the four things needed for photosynthesis.
24) What are the three variable quantities which affect the rate of photosynthesis?
25) Sketch a graph for each one and explain the shape.
26) Name and describe the three ways plants use glucose. Describe three more uses.
27) What are auxins? Where are they produced? What happens if you cut a shoot tip off?
28) Describe the three commercial uses for plant hormones.
29) Explain why water is so important to plants. Why do plants wilt when water is in short supply?
30) Name the minerals required by plants. What are they needed for? How do they get into plants?
31) What are the two types of tubes in plants? Whereabouts are they found in plants?
32) What is transpiration? What causes transpiration? What benefits does it bring?
33) What are the four factors which affect the rate of transpiration?
34) Describe what food chains and food webs are. Give two examples of both.
35) Write down 10 (or 11) technical terms for food webs (P.20) and give a definition of each one.
36) Where does the energy in a food chain originate? What happens to the energy?
37) How much energy passes from one trophic level to the next?
38) What are number pyramids? Why do you generally get a pyramid of numbers?
39) Why do number pyramids sometimes go wrong, and which pyramids are always right?
40) What is the carbon cycle all to do with? Draw as much of it from memory as you can.
41) What is the nitrogen cycle all about? Draw as much of it from memory as you can.
42) What do the four types of bacteria in the nitrogen cycle actually do?
43) Explain in detail how pesticides enter the food chain. What happened with DDT in the '60s?
44) What happens to toxin levels at each trophic level of a food chain?

Atoms

The structure of atoms is _real simple_. I mean, gee, there's nothing to them. In the past it was even easier. People thought that atoms were the _smallest things around_. But it's much more fun now we've changed all that and have protons, neutrons and electrons. Just learn and enjoy.

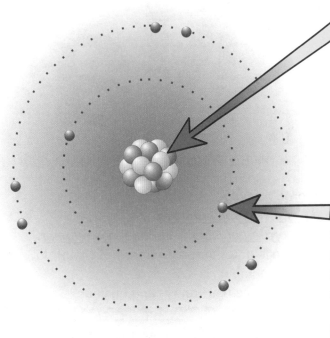

The Nucleus

1) It's in the _middle_ of the atom.
2) It contains _protons_ and _neutrons_.
3) It has a _positive charge_ because of the protons.
4) Almost the _whole_ mass of the atom is _concentrated_ in the nucleus.
5) But size-wise it's _tiny_ compared to the rest of the atom.

The Electrons

1) Move _around_ the nucleus.
2) They're _negatively charged_.
3) They're _tiny_, but they cover _a lot of space_.
4) The _volume_ their orbits occupy determines how big the atom is.
5) They have virtually _no_ mass.
6) They occupy _shells_ around the nucleus.
7) These shells explain _the whole of Chemistry_.

Atoms are _real tiny_, don't forget. They're _too small to see_, even with a microscope.

Number of Protons Equals Number of Electrons

1) Neutral atoms have _no charge_ overall.
2) The _charge_ on the electrons is the _same_ size as the charge on the _protons_ but _opposite_.
3) This means the _number_ of _protons_ always equals the _number_ of _electrons_ in a _neutral atom_.
4) If some electrons are _added or removed_, the atom becomes _charged_ and is then an _ION_.
5) The number of neutrons isn't fixed but is usually just a bit _higher_ than the number of protons.

Know Your Particles

PROTONS are _HEAVY_ and _POSITIVELY CHARGED_
NEUTRONS are _HEAVY_ and _NEUTRAL_
ELECTRONS are _Tiny_ and _NEGATIVELY CHARGED_

PARTICLE	MASS	CHARGE
Proton	1	+1
Neutron	1	0
Electron	$\frac{1}{1840}$	-1

Basic Atom facts — they don't take up much space...

This stuff on atoms should be permanently engraved in the minds of everyone.
I don't understand how people can get through the day without knowing this stuff, really I don't.
LEARN IT NOW, and watch as the Universe unfolds and reveals its timeless mysteries to you...

Atomic Number and Mass Number

Come on. These are just _two simple numbers_ for goodness' sake.
It just can't be that difficult to remember what they tell you about an atom.

THE MASS NUMBER

— Total of Protons and Neutrons
(sometimes referred to as A)

THE ATOMIC NUMBER

— Number of Protons
(sometimes called proton number,
and referred to as Z)

$$^{23}_{11}\text{Na}$$

POINTS TO NOTE

1) The _proton number_ (or _atomic number_) tells you how many _protons_ there are (oddly enough).
2) This _also_ tells you how many _electrons_ there are.
3) All atoms of the _same element_ have the _same proton number_.
4) Any atoms of two _different elements_ will have _different proton numbers_
5) To get the number of _neutrons_ — just _subtract_ the _proton number_ from the _mass number_.
6) The _mass_ number is always the _biggest_ number. It tells you the relative mass of the atom.
7) The _mass_ number is always roughly _double_ the _proton_ number.
8) Which means there's about the _same_ number of protons as neutrons in any nucleus.

Isotopes are the same except for an extra neutron or two

A favourite trick Exam question: "Explain what is meant by the term _Isotope_"
The trick is that it's impossible to explain what one isotope is. Nice of them that, isn't it!
You have to outsmart them and always start your answer _"ISOTOPES ARE..._
LEARN THE DEFINITION:

> _ISOTOPES ARE:_ different atomic forms of the _same element_, which have
> the SAME number of PROTONS but a DIFFERENT number of NEUTRONS.

1) The upshot is: isotopes must have the _same_ proton number but _different_ mass numbers.
2) _If_ they had _different_ proton numbers, they'd be _different_ elements altogether.
3) A very popular pair of isotopes are _carbon-12_ and _carbon-14_.

Carbon-12

$$^{12}_{6}\text{C}$$

6 PROTONS
6 ELECTRONS
6 NEUTRONS

Carbon-14

$$^{14}_{6}\text{C}$$

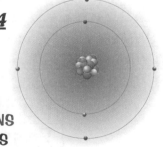

6 PROTONS
6 ELECTRONS
8 NEUTRONS

The _number_ of electrons decides the _chemistry_ of the element. If the _atomic number_ is the same (that is, the _number of protons_ is the same) then the _number of electrons_ must be the same, so the _chemistry_ is the same. The number of _neutrons_ in the nucleus _doesn't_ affect the chemical behaviour _at all_.

Learn what those blinking numbers mean...

There really isn't that much information on this page — three definitions, a couple of diagrams and a dozen or so extra details. All you gotta do is _READ IT_, _LEARN IT_, _COVER THE PAGE_ and _SCRIBBLE IT ALL DOWN AGAIN_. Smile and enjoy.

Electron Shells

The fact that electrons occupy "shells" around the nucleus is what causes the whole of chemistry. Remember that, and watch how it applies to each bit of it. It's ace.

Electron Shell Rules:

1) Electrons always occupy _SHELLS_ (sometimes called _ENERGY LEVELS_).
2) The _LOWEST_ energy levels are _ALWAYS FILLED FIRST_.
3) Only _a certain number_ of electrons are allowed in each shell:
1st shell: 2   _2nd Shell:_ 8   _3rd Shell:_ 8
(You don't need to know the numbers for the other shells)
4) Atoms are much _HAPPIER_ when they have _FULL electron shells_.
5) In most atoms the _OUTER SHELL_ is _NOT FULL_ and this makes the atom want to _REACT_.
6) We always write the shell numbers with dots between them. So argon, with it's three full shells, is 2.8.8

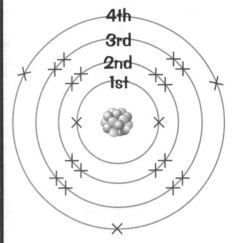

4th shell still filling

Dot and Cross diagrams

A _"Dot and Cross"_ diagram is a picture of the shells of two or more atoms, usually shown reacting, with the _electrons_ on one drawn as _crosses_, on the other drawn as _dots_. Simple, huh? Here's an example:

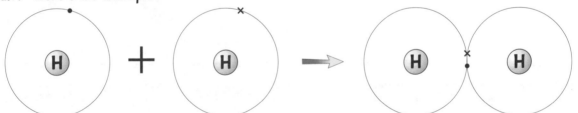

Working out Electron Configurations

You need to know the _electron configurations_ for the first _20_ elements. But they're not hard to work out. For a quick example, take nitrogen. _Follow the steps..._

1) The periodic table (see the inside front cover) tells us nitrogen has _seven_ protons... so it must have _seven_ electrons.
2) Follow the _'Electron Shell Rules'_ above. The _first_ shell can only take 2 electrons and the _second_ shell can take a _maximum_ of 8 electrons.
3) So the electron configuration for nitrogen _must_ be _2.5_. Easy peasy.
4) Now _you_ try it for chlorine.

> _Answer..._ To calculate the electron configuration of chlorine, _follow the rules_. It's got 17 protons, so it _must_ have 17 electrons. The first shell must have _2_ electrons, the second shell must have _8_, and so there are _7_ left for the third shell. It's as easy as _2.8.7_.

Electrons rule...

There's some _really important stuff_ on this page and you _really do_ need to _learn all of it_. Once you have, it'll make all of the rest of the stuff in this book an awful lot _easier_. Practise calculating _electron configurations_ and drawing _electron shell_ diagrams.

Ionic Bonding

Ionic Bonding — Swapping Electrons

In _IONIC BONDING_, atoms _lose or gain electrons_ to form _charged particles_ (ions) which are then _strongly attracted_ to one another, (the attraction of opposite charges, + and –).

A shell with just one electron is well keen to get rid...

All the atoms over at the _left hand side_ of the periodic table, such as _sodium, potassium, calcium_ etc. have just _one or two electrons_ in their outer shell. And basically they're _pretty keen to get shot of them_, because then they'll only have _full shells_ left, which is how they _like_ it. So given half a chance they do get rid, and that leaves the atom as an _ION_ instead. Now ions aren't the kind of things that sit around quietly watching the world go by. They tend to _leap_ at the first passing ion with an _opposite charge_ and stick to it like glue.

A nearly full shell is well keen to get that extra electron...

On the _other side_ of the periodic table, the elements in _group six_ and _group seven_, such as _oxygen_ and _chlorine_ have outer shells which are _nearly full_. They're obviously pretty keen to _gain_ that _extra one or two electrons_ to fill the shell up. When they do of course they become _IONS_, you know, not the kind of things to sit around, and before you know it, _POP_, they've latched onto the atom (now an ion) that gave up the electron a moment earlier. The reaction of sodium and chlorine is a _classic case_:

The _sodium_ atom _gives up_ its _outer electron_ and becomes an Na$^+$ ion.

The _chlorine_ atom _picks up_ the _spare electron_ and becomes a Cl$^-$ ion.

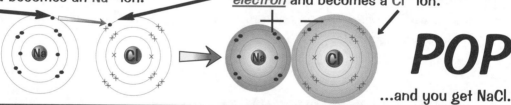

POP!

...and you get NaCl.

Giant Ionic Structures don't melt easily, but when they do...

1) _Ionic bonds_ always produce _giant ionic structures_, held together by the attraction of _opposite charges_.
2) The ions form a _closely packed_ regular lattice arrangement.
3) There are _very strong_ chemical bonds between _all_ the ions.
4) A single crystal of salt is _one giant ionic lattice_, which is why salt crystals tend to be cuboid in shape.

1) They have _High melting points and boiling points_

due to the _very strong_ chemical bonds between _all the ions_ in the giant structure.

2) They _Dissolve to form solutions that conduct electricity_

most will dissolve in water, and _when dissolved_ the ions _separate_ and are all _free to move_ in the solution, so obviously they'll _carry electric current_.

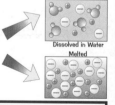
Dissolved in Water
Melted

3) They _Conduct electricity when molten_

When it _melts_, the ions are _free to move_ and they'll carry electric current.

Full shells — it's the name of the game, pal...

Make sure you know exactly _how_ and _why_ ionic bonds are formed. There's quite a lot of words on this page but only to hammer home _three basic points_: 1) Ionic bonds involve _swapping_ electrons   2) Some atoms like to _lose_ them, some like to _gain_ them   3) Ionic bonds lead to the formation of giant ionic structures. Learn _all_ the features of giant ionic structures.

Electron Shells and Ions

Simple Ions — Groups 1 & 2 and 6 & 7

1) Remember, atoms that have _lost_ or _gained_ an electron (or electrons) are _ions_.
2) The elements that most readily form ions are those in Groups 1, 2, 6, and 7.
3) _Group 1 and 2 elements_ are _metals_ and they _lose_ electrons to form _+ve ions_ or _cations_.
4) _Group 6 and 7 elements_ are _non-metals_. They _gain_ electrons to form _–ve ions_ or _anions_.
5) Make sure you know these easy ones:

CATIONS		ANIONS	
Gr I	Gr II	Gr VI	Gr VII
Li$^+$	Be^{2+}	O^{2-}	F$^-$
Na$^+$	Mg^{2+}	Cl$^-$	
K$^+$	Ca^{2+}		

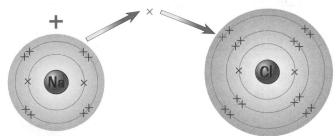

6) When any of the above elements _react together_, they form _ionic bonds_.
7) Only elements at _opposite sides_ of the periodic table will form ionic bonds, e.g. Na and Cl, where one of them becomes a _CATION_ (+ve) and one becomes an _ANION_ (–ve).

> Remember, the + and – charges we talk about, e.g. Na$^+$ for sodium, just tell you what type of ion the atom WILL FORM in a chemical reaction. In sodium _metal_ there are _only neutral sodium atoms, Na_. The Na$^+$ ions _will only appear_ if the sodium metal _reacts_ with something like water or chlorine.

Electronic structure of some simple ions

A useful way of representing ions is by specifying the _ion's name_, followed by its _electron configuration_ and the _charge_ on the ion. For example, the electronic structure of the sodium ion Na$^+$ can be represented by $[2,8]^+$. That's the electron configuration followed by the charge on the ion. Simple enough. A few _ions_ and the _ionic compounds_ they form are shown below.

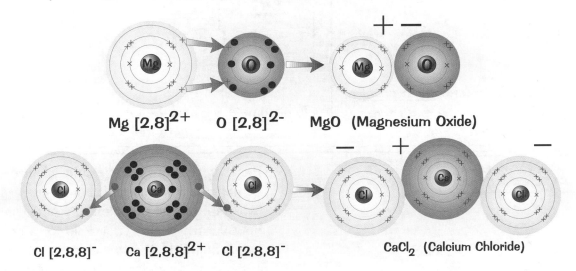

Mg $[2,8]^{2+}$ O $[2,8]^{2-}$ MgO (Magnesium Oxide)

Cl $[2,8,8]^-$ Ca $[2,8,8]^{2+}$ Cl $[2,8,8]^-$ CaCl$_2$ (Calcium Chloride)

Simple ions — looks simple enough to me...

Yet again, more stuff you've _got_ to know. _LEARN_ which atoms form 1+, 1-, 2+ and 2- ions, and why. You need to know how to represent ions _both_ in [x,y] notation _and_ by diagrams. When you think you've got it, _cover the page_ and start scribbling to see what you really know. Then look back, _learn the bits you missed_, and _try again_. And again.

Covalent Bonding

Covalent Bonds — Sharing Electrons

1) Sometimes atoms prefer to make _COVALENT BONDS_ by _sharing_ electrons with other atoms.
2) This way _both_ atoms feel that they have a _full outer shell_, and that makes them happy.
3) Each _single covalent bond_ provides one _extra_ shared electron for each atom.
4) Each atom involved has to make _enough_ covalent bonds to _fill up_ its outer shell.

5) _LEARN_ these _FIVE IMPORTANT EXAMPLES_:

1) Hydrogen Gas, H₂

Hydrogen atoms have just one electron. They _only need one more_ to complete the first shell...

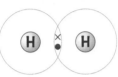

Or

H—H

...so they often form _single covalent bonds_ to achieve this.

2) Chlorine Gas, Cl₂

This is very similar to H₂. Again, both atoms _only need one more electron_ to complete their outer shells.

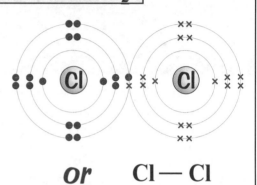

Or   Cl—Cl

3) Ammonia, NH₃

Nitrogen has _five_ outer electrons...

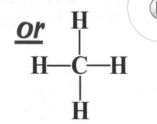

or

H
|
H—N—H

...so it needs to form _three covalent bonds_ to make up the extra _three_ electrons needed.

4) Methane, CH₄

Carbon has _four outer electrons_, which is a _half-full_ shell.

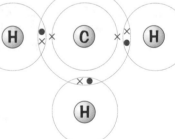

or

H
|
H—C—H
|
H

To become a 4+ or a 4− ion is hard work so it forms _four covalent bonds_ to make up its outer shell.

5) Water, H₂O

or

O
H   H

The _oxygen_ atom has _six_ outer electrons. Sometimes it forms _ionic_ bonds by _taking_ two electrons to complete the outer shell. However it will also cheerfully form _covalent bonds_ and _SHARE_ two electrons instead, as in the case of _water molecules_, where it _shares_ electrons with the H atoms.

Full shells — you just can't beat them...

LEARN the four numbered points about covalent bonds and the five examples.
Then turn over and scribble it all down again. Make sure you can draw all five molecules and explain exactly why they form the bonds that they do. _All from memory of course_.

Double Covalent Bonds

Double Covalent Bonds — Sharing more Electrons

1) Sometimes atoms will form _double_ covalent bonds.
2) In these each atom _contributes two electrons_ to each bond it forms.
3) So _two pairs_ of electrons are in each bond.
4) Again, each atom has to make enough covalent bonds to _fill up_ its outer shell.
5) It can do this with just one type of covalent bond, or with some single _and_ some double bonds.
6) _LEARN_ these three _Earth shatteringly important examples_:

1) Oxygen Gas, O_2

Oxygen needs _two_ more electrons to fill its outer shell.

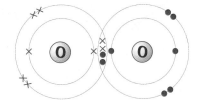

So a _double bond_ does the job nicely.

_or_

$$O=O$$

2) Carbon dioxide, CO_2

Carbon has four outer shell electrons, so it needs _four more_ to fill its second shell. Oxygen needs _two more_, so carbon can satisfy two oxygen atoms with double bonds.

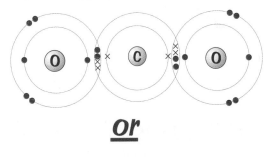

_or_

$$O=C=O$$

3) Ethene, C_2H_4

A substance can have _both_ single and double bonds.

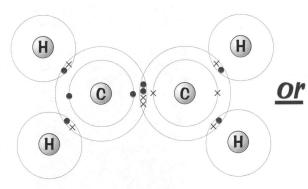

_or_

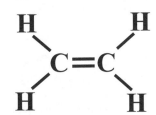

Hydrogen needs just one more electron to fill its outer shell, so it's _not interested_ in forming a double bond, just a single bond. But by hook or by crook, carbon wants to get _FOUR_ more electrons...

...so sometimes, it'll form some _single bonds_ with hydrogen, and a _double bond_ with another carbon atom, to create _ethene_ (see P. 64, Volume 1).

It's a _bit_ more complicated, but it's not really any harder. Each carbon atom shares _two_ of its electrons with the other carbon, and shares _one_ of its electrons with each of two hydrogen atoms. In return it gets the same back, and everything has _full shells_ and is happy.

The name's Bond — Double Bond...

There's not really much different to understand with these. They're a push-over as long as you _understand_ single bonds. So you'd better make sure you do. And you're gonna have to be able to remember these _three examples_, and the numbered points at the top. So get _scribbling_...

Covalent Substances: Two Kinds

Substances formed from _covalent bonds_ can either be _simple molecules_ or _giant structures_.

Simple Molecular Substances

1) The atoms form _very strong_ covalent bonds to form _small_ molecules of several atoms.
2) By contrast, the forces of attraction _between_ these molecules are _very weak_.
3) The result of these feeble _inter-molecular forces_ is that the _melting_ and _boiling points_ are _very low_, because the molecules are _easily parted_ from each other.
4) Most molecular substances are _gases or liquids_ at room temperature.
5) Molecular substances _don't conduct electricity_, simply because there are _no ions_.
6) They _don't dissolve in water_, usually.
7) You can usually tell a molecular substance just from its _physical state_, which is always kinda '_mushy_' — i.e. _liquid_ or _gas_ or an _easily-melted solid_.

Very weak inter-molecular forces

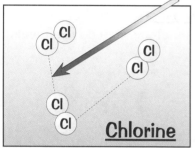
Chlorine

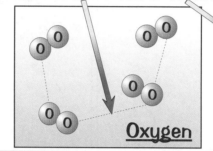
Oxygen

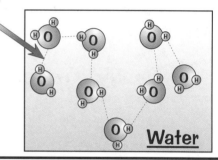
Water

Giant Covalent Structures

1) These are similar to giant ionic structures except that there are _no charged ions_.
2) _All_ the atoms are _bonded_ to _each other_ by _strong_ covalent bonds.
3) They have _very high_ melting and boiling points.
4) They _don't conduct electricity_ — not even when _molten_.
5) They're usually _insoluble_ in water.
6) The _main examples_ are _diamond_ and _graphite_ which are both made only from _carbon atoms_.

Diamond

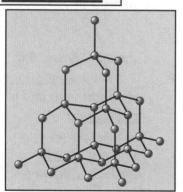

Each carbon atom forms _four covalent bonds_ in a _very rigid_ giant covalent structure.

Graphite

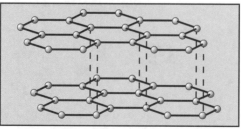

Each carbon atom only forms _three covalent bonds_, creating _layers_ which are free to _slide over each other_, and leaving _free electrons_, so graphite is unlike most _non-metals_, and _conducts electricity_.

Silicon Dioxide

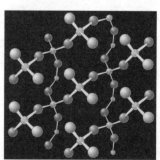

Sometimes called _silica_, this is what _sand_ is made of.
Each grain of sand is _one giant structure_ of silicon and oxygen.

Come on — pull yourself together...

There are two types of covalently bonded substances — and they're totally different. Make sure you know all the details about them and the examples too. _This is real basic stuff_ — just easy marks to be won... or lost. _Cover the page_ and see how many marks you're gonna _WIN_.

Relative Formula Mass

The biggest trouble with *RELATIVE ATOMIC MASS* and *RELATIVE FORMULA MASS* is that they *sound* so bloodcurdling. *"With big scary names like that they must be really, really complicated."* I hear you cry. Nope, wrong. They're dead easy. Take a few deep breaths, and just enjoy, as the mists slowly clear...

Relative Atomic Mass, A_r — easy peasy

1) This is just a way of saying how *heavy* different atoms are *compared to each other*.
2) The *relative atomic mass* A_r is nothing more than the *mass number* of the element.
3) On the periodic table, the elements all have *two* numbers. The smaller one is the atomic number (how many protons it has).
But the *bigger one* is the *mass number* (how many protons and neutrons it has)
which, kind of obviously, is also the *Relative atomic mass*. Easy peasy, I'd say.

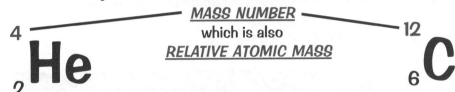

MASS NUMBER
which is also
RELATIVE ATOMIC MASS

$$_2^4 He \qquad\qquad _6^{12} C$$

Helium has $A_r = 4$. Carbon has $A_r = 12$. (So carbon atoms are *3 times heavier* than helium atoms)

Relative Formula Mass, M_r — also easy peasy

If you have a compound like $MgCl_2$ then it has a *RELATIVE FORMULA MASS*, M_r, which is just all the relative atomic masses *added together*.
For $MgCl_2$ it would be:

$$Mg\ Cl_2$$

$$24 \quad + \quad (35.5 \times 2) \quad = \quad 95$$

So the M_r for $MgCl_2$ is simply <u>95</u>.

You can easily get the A_r for any element from the *periodic table* (see inside front cover), but in a lot of questions they give you them anyway.
I tell you what, since it's nearly Christmas I'll run through another example for you:

<u>Question:</u> *Find the relative formula mass for calcium carbonate, $CaCO_3$ using the given data:*
A_r for Ca = 40 A_r for C = 12 A_r for O = 16

ANSWER:

$$CaCO_3$$

$$40 \quad + \quad 12 \quad + \quad (16 \times 3) \quad = 100$$

So the Relative Formula Mass for $CaCO_3$ is <u>100</u>.

And that's all it is. A big fancy name like *Relative Formula Mass* and all it means is *"add up all the mass numbers"*. What a swizz, eh? You'd have thought it'd be something a bit juicier than that, wouldn't you. Still, that's life — it's all a big disappointment in the end. Sigh.

Phew, Chemistry — scary stuff sometimes, innit...

When you know it, <u>cover the page</u> and <u>scribble down</u> the important details. Did ya miss any?
1) Use the periodic table to find the relative atomic mass of these elements: Cu, K, Kr, Fe, Cl
2) Also find the relative formula mass of these compounds: NaOH, Fe_2O_3, C_6H_{14}, $Mg(NO_3)_2$

Two Formula Mass Calculations

Although Relative Atomic Mass and Relative Formula Mass are *easy enough*, it can get just a tadge *trickier* when you start getting into other calculations which use them. It depends on how good your maths is basically, because it's all to do with ratios and percentages.

Calculating % Mass of an Element in a Compound

This is actually dead easy — so long as you've learnt this formula:

$$\text{PERCENTAGE MASS OF AN ELEMENT IN A COMPOUND} = \frac{A_r \times \text{No. of atoms (of that element)}}{M_r \text{ (of whole compound)}} \times 100$$

If you don't learn the formula then you'd better be pretty smart — or you'll struggle.

EXAMPLE: Find the percentage mass of sodium in sodium carbonate, Na_2CO_3
ANSWER:

A_r of sodium = 23, Ar of carbon =12, Ar of oxygen =16
M_r of Na_2CO_3 = $(2\times23)+12+(3\times16)=106$

Now use the formula:

$$\text{Percentage mass} = \frac{A_r \times n}{M_r} \times 100 = \frac{23 \times 2}{106} \times 100 = 43.4\%$$

And there you have it. Sodium represents *43.4%* of the mass of sodium carbonate.

Finding the Empirical Formula (from Masses or Percentages)

This also sounds a lot worse than it really is. Try this for an easy peasy *stepwise method*:

1) *LIST ALL THE ELEMENTS* in the compound (there's usually only two or three!)
2) *Underneath them*, write their *EXPERIMENTAL MASSES OR PERCENTAGES*.
3) *DIVIDE* each mass or percentage *BY THE* A_r for that particular element.
4) Turn the numbers you get into *A NICE SIMPLE RATIO* by multiplying and/or dividing them by well-chosen numbers.
5) Get the ratio in its *SIMPLEST FORM*, and that tells you the formula of the compound.

EXAMPLE: Find the empirical formula of the iron oxide produced when 44.8g of iron react with 19.2g of oxygen. (A_r for iron = 56, A_r for oxygen =16)
METHOD:

	Fe	O
1) List the two elements:	Fe	O
2) Write in the *experimental masses*:	44.8	19.2
3) Divide by the A_r for each element:	$44.8/56 = 0.8$	$19.2/16 = 1.2$
4) Multiply by 10...	8	12
...then divide by 4:	2	3

5) So the *simplest formula* is 2 atoms of Fe to 3 atoms of O, i.e. Fe_2O_3. And that's it done.

> You need to realise (for the Exam) that this *EMPIRICAL METHOD* (i.e. based on *experiment*) is the *only way* of finding out the formula of a compound. Rust is iron oxide, sure, but is it FeO, or Fe_2O_3? Only an experiment to determine the empirical formula will tell you for certain.

Old Dmitri Mendeleev did this sort of stuff in his sleep — the old rogue...

Make sure you *learn the formula* at the top and the five rules in the box. Then try these:
1) Find the percentage mass of oxygen in these: a) Fe_2O_3 b) H_2O c) $CaCO_3$ d) H_2SO_4
2) Find the empirical formula when 2.4g of carbon reacts with 0.8g of hydrogen.

Calculating Volumes

These are OK as long as you *LEARN* the formula in the *RED BOX* and know how to use it.

1) Calculating the Volume *when you know the Masses*

For this type of question there are *TWO STAGES*:

1) *Find the reacting mass*, exactly like in the examples on the last page.
2) Then *convert the mass into a volume* using this formula:

$$\frac{\text{VOL. OF GAS (in cm}^3\text{)}}{24,000} = \frac{\text{MASS OF GAS}}{M_r \text{ of gas}}$$

This formula comes from the well known(!) fact that:

A MASS OF M_r IN GRAMS, of any gas, will always occupy *24 LITRES*
(at room temperature and pressure) — and it's the same for *ANY GAS*.

I reckon it's easier to learn and use the formula, but it's certainly worth knowing that fact too.

EXAMPLE: Find the volume of carbon dioxide produced (at room T and P) when 2.7g of carbon is completely burned in oxygen. (A_r of carbon = 12, A_r of oxygen = 16)

ANSWER:

1) Balanced equation:
2) Fill in M_r for each:
3) Divide for one, times for all:

$$C + O_2 \rightarrow CO_2$$

	12	32	44	
÷12	1	....	3.6666667	÷12
×2.7	2.7	....	9.8999999	×2.7

4) So 2.7g of C gives 9.9g of CO_2.
   Now the new bit:

$$= \underline{9.9}$$

5) *USING THE ABOVE FORMULA:*

$$\frac{\text{Volume}}{24,000} = \frac{\text{MASS}}{M_r}$$ $$\text{Volume} = \frac{\text{MASS}}{M_r} \times 24,000$$

so Volume = (MASS/M_r) × 24,000 = (9.9/44) × 24000 = [5400.] = $\underline{5400 \text{cm}^3}$ or $\underline{5.40 \text{ litres}}$.

2) Calculating the Mass *when you're given the Volume*

For this type of question the *TWO STAGES* are in the *reverse order*:

1) First *find the mass from the volume* using the same formula as before:

$$\frac{\text{VOL. OF GAS (in cm}^3\text{)}}{24,000} = \frac{\text{MASS OF GAS}}{M_r \text{ of gas}}$$

2) Then *find the reacting mass*, exactly like in the examples on the last page.

EXAMPLE: Find the mass of 6.2 litres of oxygen gas. (A_r of oxygen = 16)

ANSWER: Using the above formula: $$\frac{6,200}{24,000} = \frac{\text{Mass of Gas}}{32}$$

(Look out, 32, because it's O_2)

Hence,   Mass of Gas = (6,200/24,000) × 32 = [8.2666667] = $\underline{8.27\text{g}}$

The question would likely go on to ask what mass of CO_2 would be produced if this much oxygen reacted with carbon. In that case you would now just apply the same old method from the previous page (as used above).

Calculating volumes — it's just a gas...

Make sure you *learn the formula* in the red box at the top and that you know how to use it.
1) Find the volume of 2.5g of methane gas, CH_4. (at room T & P).
2) Find the mass of oxide (MgO) produced when magnesium is burned with 1.7 litres of oxygen.

The Mole

The Mole is really confusing. I think it's the word that puts people off. It's very difficult to see the relevance of the word "mole" to different-sized piles of brightly-coloured powders.

"THE MOLE" is simply the name given to a certain number

Just like "*a million*" is this many: 1,000,000; or "*a billion*" is this many: 1,000,000,000,
so "*A MOLE*" is this many: 602,300,000,000,000,000,000,000   or 6.023×10^{23}.

1) And that's all it is. *Just a number*. The burning question, of course, is why is it such a silly long one like that, and with a six at the front?

2) The answer is that when you get *precisely that number* of atoms or molecules, *of any element or compound*, then, conveniently, they *weigh* exactly the same number of *grams* as the Relative Atomic Mass, A_r (or M_r) of the element (or compound).
This is arranged *on purpose* of course, to make things easier.

> *ONE MOLE* of atoms or molecules of any substance will have *a mass in grams* equal to the *Relative Formula Mass* (A_r or M_r) for that substance.

EXAMPLES:

Carbon has an A_r of 12.   So one mole of carbon weighs exactly 12g.
Nitrogen gas, N_2, has an M_r of 28 (2×14).   So one mole of N_2 weighs exactly 28g
Carbon dioxide, CO_2, has an M_r of 44.   So one mole of CO_2 weighs exactly 44g

This means that 12g of carbon, or 28g of N_2, or 44g of CO_2, all contain the same number of atoms, namely *ONE MOLE* or 6×10^{23} atoms or molecules.

Nice Easy Formula for finding the Number of Moles in a given mass:

$$\text{NUMBER OF MOLES} = \frac{\text{Mass in g} \quad \text{(of element or compound)}}{M_r \quad \text{(of element or compound)}}$$

EXAMPLE: How many moles are there in 42g of carbon?
ANSWER: No. of moles = Mass (g) / M_r = 42/12 = *3.5 moles*.   Easy Peasy.

"Relative Formula Mass" is also "Molar Mass"

1) We've been very happy using the Relative Formula Mass, M_r all through the calculations.
2) In fact, that was already using the idea of Moles because M_r is actually the mass of one mole in g, or as we sometimes call it, the *MOLAR MASS*.
3) It follows that *the volume of one mole of any gas* will be *24 litres* — *THE MOLAR VOLUME*.

A "One Molar Solution" Contains "One Mole per Litre"

This is pretty easy. So a 2M solution of NaOH contains 2 moles of NaOH per litre of solution. Since a litre is a dm^3, sometimes people will say a 1M solution has a concentration of 1 mol/dm^3 You need to know how many moles there'll be in a given volume:

$$\text{NUMBER OF MOLES} = \textit{VOLUME} \text{ in Litres} \times \textit{MOLARITY} \text{ of solution}$$

EXAMPLE: How many moles in 185cm^3 of a 2M solution?   *ANS:* $0.185 \times 2 = $ *0.37 moles*

Moles — a suitably silly name for such a confusing idea...

It's possible to do all the calculations on the previous pages without ever talking about moles. You just concentrate on M_r and A_r all the time instead. In fact M_r and A_r represent moles anyway, but *I* think it's less confusing if moles aren't mentioned at all.

Calculating Masses in Reactions

These can be kinda scary too, but chill out, my young friend — just relax and enjoy.
It all works because *mass* is always *conserved*. In fact *atoms* are conserved — the number of atoms on the two sides of the reaction is *always* the same for each type of atom.

The Three Important Steps — *not to be missed...*

(Miss one out and it'll all go horribly wrong, believe me)

> 1) *WRITE OUT* the balanced *EQUATION*
> 2) *Work out* M_r — just for the *TWO BITS YOU WANT*
> 3) Apply the rule: *DIVIDE TO GET ONE, THEN MULTIPLY TO GET ALL*
>
> (But you have to apply this first to the substance they give
> information about, and *then* the other one!)

EXAMPLE: *What mass of magnesium oxide is produced when 60g of magnesium is burned in air?*

ANSWER:

1) *Write out the BALANCED EQUATION:*

$$2Mg + O_2 \rightarrow 2MgO$$

2) *Work out the RELATIVE FORMULA MASSES:*

(don't do the oxygen — we don't need it)

$$2 \times 24 \rightarrow 2 \times (24+16)$$
$$48 \rightarrow 80$$

3) Apply the rule: *DIVIDE TO GET ONE, THEN MULTIPLY TO GET ALL*
The two numbers, 48 and 80, tell us that *48g of Mg react to give 80g of MgO.*
Here's the tricky bit. You've now got to be able to write this down:

> 48g of Mg ......reacts to give.....80g of MgO
>
> 1g of Mg ......reacts to give.....
>
> 60g of Mg .....reacts to give......

THE BIG CLUE is that in the question they've said we want to burn *"60g of magnesium"*
i.e. they've told us how much *magnesium* to have, and that's how you know to write down the
LEFT HAND SIDE of it first, because:

We'll first need to ÷ by 48 to get 1g of Mg
and then need to × by 60 to get 60g of Mg.

THEN you can work out the numbers on the other side (shown in orange below) by realising that
you must *divide BOTH sides by 48* and then *multiply BOTH sides by 60*. It's tricky.

÷48 { 48g of Mg .... 80g of MgO } ÷48
    { 1g of Mg .... 1.67g of MgO }
×60 { 60g of Mg .... 100g of MgO } ×60

You should realise that *in practise* 100% yield may not be obtained in some reactions, so the amount of product might be *slightly less than calculated*.

This finally tells us that *60g of magnesium will produce 100g of magnesium oxide*.
If the question had said "Find how much magnesium gives 500g of magnesium oxide.", you'd fill in
the MgO side first instead, *because that's the one you'd have the information about*. Got it? Good-O!

Reaction mass calculations? — *no worries, matey...*

Learn the three rules in the red box and practise the example till you can do it fluently.
1) Find the mass of calcium which gives 30g of calcium oxide (CaO), when burnt in air.

Simple Reversible Reactions

A _reversible reaction_ is one which can go _in both directions_.
In other words the _products_ of the reaction can be _turned back_ into the original _reactants_.
Generally you end up with some of one side and some of the other, not all one side and none of the other. What the _proportions_ are depends on conditions such as _temperature_ and _pressure_.
Here are some _examples_ you should know about in case they spring one on you in the Exam.

The Thermal decomposition of Ammonium Chloride

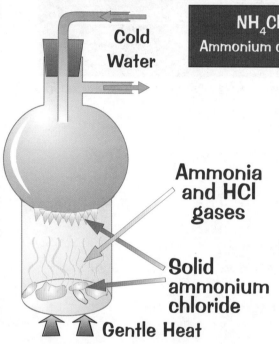

$$NH_4Cl_{(s)} \rightleftharpoons NH_{3(g)} + HCl_{(g)}$$
Ammonium chloride   ammonia   +   hydrogen chloride

Cold Water

Ammonia and HCl gases

Solid ammonium chloride

Gentle Heat

1) When _ammonium chloride_ is _heated_ it splits up into _ammonia gas_ and _HCl gas_.

2) When these gases _cool_ they recombine to form _solid ammonium chloride_.

3) This is a _typical reversible reaction_ because the products _recombine_ to form the original substance _very easily_.

The Thermal decomposition of Hydrated Copper Sulphate

1) Good old dependable _blue copper(II) sulphate_ crystals here again.

2) Here they're displaying their usual trick, but under the guise of a _reversible reaction_.

3) If you _heat them_ it drives the water off and leaves _white anhydrous_ copper(II) sulphate powder.

Water vapour

4) If you then _add_ a couple of drops of _water_ to the _white powder_ you get the _blue crystals_ back again.

The proper name for the _blue crystals_ is _hydrated copper(II) sulphate_. "_Hydrated_" means "_with water_".
When you drive the water off they become a white powder, _anhydrous copper(II) sulphate_. "_Anhydrous_" means "_without water_".

Learn these simple reactions, then see what you know...

These reactions might seem a bit obscure but it's all mentioned in the syllabus, so any of them could come up in your Exam. There really isn't much to learn here. _Scribble it._

Reversible Reactions in Equilibrium

A _reversible reaction_ is one where the _products_ can react with each other and _convert back_ to the original chemicals. In other words, _it can go both ways_.

> A _REVERSIBLE REACTION_ IS ONE WHERE THE _PRODUCTS_ OF THE REACTION CAN _THEMSELVES REACT_ TO PRODUCE THE _ORIGINAL REACTANTS_
>
> $$A + B \rightleftharpoons C + D$$

Reversible Reactions will reach Dynamic Equilibrium

1) If a reversible reaction takes place in a _closed system_ then a state of _equilibrium_ will always be reached.

2) _Equilibrium_ means that the _relative (%) quantities_ of reactants and products will reach a certain _balance_ and stay there. A _'closed system'_ just means that none of the reactants or products can _escape_.

3) It is in fact a DYNAMIC _EQUILIBRIUM_, which means that the reactions are still taking place in _both directions_ but the _overall effect is nil_ because the forward and reverse reactions _cancel_ each other out.

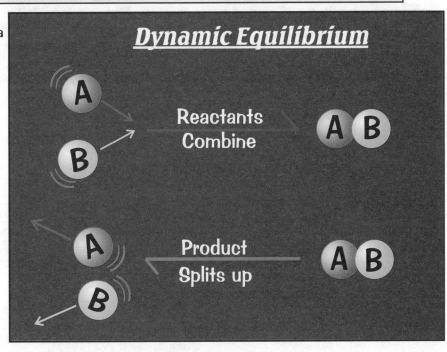

Dynamic Equilibrium

Reactants Combine

Product Splits up

The reactions are taking place at _exactly the same rate_ in both directions.

Changing Temperature and Pressure to get More Product

1) In a reversible reaction the _'position of equilibrium'_ (the relative amounts of reactants and products) depends _very strongly_ on the _temperature_ and _pressure_ surrounding the reaction.

2) If we _deliberately alter_ the temperature and pressure (or concentration) we can _move_ the "position of equilibrium" to give _more product_ and _less_ reactants.

Two very simple rules for which way the equilibrium will move

1) All reactions are _exothermic_ in one direction and _endothermic_ in the other.
   If we _raise_ the _temperature_, the _endothermic_ reaction will increase to _use up_ the extra heat.
   If we _reduce_ the _temperature_ the _exothermic_ reaction will increase to _give out_ more heat.

2) Many reactions have a _greater volume_ on one side, either of _products_ or _reactants_.
   If we _raise_ the _pressure_ it will encourage the reaction which produces _less volume_.
   If we _lower_ the _pressure_ it will encourage the reaction which produces _more volume_.

Learning/forgetting— the worst reversible of them all...

There's three sections here: the definition of a reversible reaction, the notion of dynamic equilibrium and ways to get more product. Make sure you can give a good rendition of all three.

The Haber Process

This is an *important industrial process*. It produces *ammonia* which is needed for making *fertilisers*.

Nitrogen and Hydrogen are needed to make Ammonia

1) The *nitrogen* is obtained easily from the *AIR*, which is *78% nitrogen* (and 21% oxygen).
2) The *hydrogen* is obtained from *WATER* (steam) and *NATURAL GAS* (methane, CH_4).
   The methane and steam are reacted *together* like this:

$$CH_{4\,(g)} + H_2O_{(g)} \rightarrow CO_{(g)} + 3H_{2\,(g)}$$

3) Hydrogen can also be obtained from *crude oil*.

The Haber Process is a Reversible Reaction:

$$N_{2\,(g)} + 3H_{2\,(g)} \rightleftharpoons 2NH_{3\,(g)} \quad (+ \text{ heat})$$

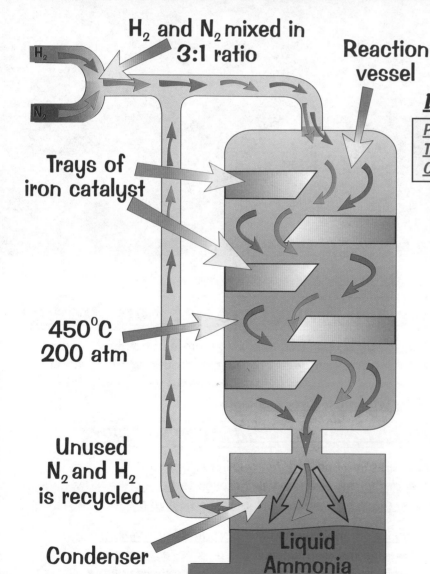

H₂ and N₂ mixed in 3:1 ratio

Reaction vessel

Trays of iron catalyst

450°C 200 atm

Unused N₂ and H₂ is recycled

Condenser

Liquid Ammonia

Industrial conditions:

PRESSURE:	200 atmospheres
TEMPERATURE:	450°C
CATALYST:	Iron

EXTRA NOTES:

1) The hydrogen and nitrogen are mixed together in a *3:1 ratio*.

2) Because the reaction is *reversible*, not all of the nitrogen and hydrogen will *convert* to ammonia.

3) The *ammonia* is formed as a *gas* but as it cools in the condenser it *liquefies* and is *removed*.

4) The N₂ and H₂ which didn't react are *recycled* and passed through again so *none is wasted*.

200 atmospheres? — that could give you a headache...

There are quite a lot of details on this page. They're pretty keen on the Haber process in the Exams so you'd be well advised to learn all this. They could easily ask you on any of these details. Use the same good old method: *Learn it, cover it up, repeat it back to yourself, check, try again...*

The Haber Process

Higher Pressure will Favour the Forward Reaction so build it strong...

1) On the _left side_ of the equation there are _four moles_ of gas (N_2 + $3H_2$), whilst on the _right side_ there are just _two moles_ (of NH_3).

2) So any _increase_ in _pressure_ will favour the _forward reaction_ to produce more _ammonia_. Hence the decision on pressure is _simple_. It's just set _as high as possible_ to give the _best %_ _yield_ without making the plant _too expensive_ to build. 200 to 350 atmospheres are typical pressures used.

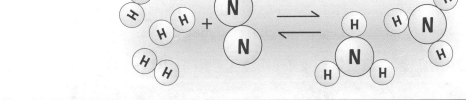

Lower Temperature WOULD favour the forward Reaction BUT...

The reaction is _exothermic_ in the forward direction which means that _increasing_ the temperature will actually move the equilibrium _the wrong way_, away from ammonia and more towards H_2 and N_2. But they _increase_ the temperature anyway... this is the tricky bit so learn it real good:

1) The _proportion_ of ammonia at equilibrium can be increased by _lowering_ the temperature.

2) But instead they _raise_ the temperature and accept a _reduced_ proportion (or _yield_) of ammonia.

3) The reason is that the _higher_ temperature gives a much higher _RATE OF REACTION_.

4) It's better to wait _20 seconds_ for a _10% yield_ than to have to wait _60 seconds_ for a _20% yield_.

5) Remember, the unused hydrogen, H_2, and nitrogen, N_2, are _recycled_ so _nothing is wasted_.

The Iron Catalyst Speeds up the reaction and keeps costs down

1) The _iron catalyst_ makes the reaction go _quicker_ which gets it to the _equilibrium proportions_ more quickly. But don't forget that the catalyst _doesn't_ affect the _position_ of equilibrium (i.e. the % yield). _Remember_ that iron is one of the _transition metals_ and that the transition metals are commonly used as catalysts.

2) _Without the catalyst_ the temperature would have to be _raised even further_ to get a _quick enoug_ reaction and that would _reduce the % yield_ even further. So the catalyst is very important.

Maximising the product is a matter of compromise

1) _Removing product_ would be an effective way to improve yield because the reaction keeps _chasing equilibrium_ while the product keeps _disappearing_. Eventually _the whole lot_ is converted.

2) This _can't be done_ in the Haber Process because the ammonia can't be removed until _afterwards_ when the mixture is _cooled_ to _condense out_ the ammonia.

3) The reaction is _exothermic_, and the heat given out is used to heat up _fresh supplies_ of nitrogen and hydrogen (_before_ they enter the reaction vessel) to _speed up_ their rate of reaction.

4) Ammonia is rather _important_ stuff. It's used for making ammonium nitrate _fertiliser_, which is pretty important to ensure that we all get enough to eat. This explains why the Haber process is so important, and why _you_ have to learn so much about it.

Learning the Haber process — it's all ebb and flow...

If they're going to use any reversible reaction for an Exam question, the chances are its going to be this one. The trickiest bit is that the temperature is raised not for a better equilibrium, but for increased speed. Try the mini-essay method to _scribble down all you know_ about equilibrium and the Haber process.

Fertiliser from Ammonia

Reversible Reactions

On this page are *two reactions* involving *ammonia* that you need to be familiar with. Somehow, I don't think I'd have either of them in my list of "Top Ten Most Riveting Chemistry Topics":

1) Ammonia can be Oxidised to form Nitric Acid

There are *two stages* to this reaction:

a) Ammonia gas reacts with oxygen over a hot platinum catalyst:

$$4NH_{3\,(g)} + 5O_{2\,(g)} \rightarrow 4NO_{(g)} + 6H_2O_{(g)}$$

This first stage is very *exothermic* and produces its own heat to *keep it going*.
The nitrogen monoxide must be *cooled* before the next stage, which happens easily:

b) The nitrogen monoxide reacts with water and oxygen...

$$6NO_{(g)} + 3O_{2\,(g)} + 2H_2O_{(g)} \rightarrow 4HNO_{3\,(g)} + 2NO_{(g)}$$

...to form nitric acid, HNO_3

Gripping stuff. Anyway, the *nitric acid* produced is *very useful* for other chemical processes. One such use is to make *ammonium nitrate* fertiliser...

2) Ammonia can be neutralised with Nitric Acid...

...to make Ammonium Nitrate fertiliser

This is a straightforward and spectacularly unexciting *neutralisation* reaction between an *alkali* (ammonia) and an *acid*. The result is of course a *neutral salt:* *(prod me if I fall asleep)*

$$NH_{3\,(g)} + HNO_{3\,(aq)} \rightarrow NH_4NO_{3\,(aq)}$$

Ammonia + Nitric acid → Ammonium nitrate

Ammonia can also be neutralised with *sulphuric acid*, to make *ammonium sulphate* fertiliser, but *ammonium nitrate* is an especially good fertiliser because it has *nitrogen* from *two sources*, the ammonia and the nitric acid. Kind of a *double dose*. Plants need nitrogen to make *proteins*.

Excessive Nitrate Fertiliser causes Eutrophication and Health Problems

Higher Higher Higher

1) If *nitrate fertilisers* wash into *streams* they set off a cycle of *mega-growth*, *mega-death* and *mega-decay*. Plants and green algae grow out of control, then start to *die off* because there's too many of them, then *bacteria* take over, feeding off the dying plants and using up all the *oxygen* in the water. Then the fish all die because they can't get enough *oxygen*. Lovely. It's called *eutrophication*. It's all good clean fun.
2) If too many *nitrates* get into drinking water it can cause *health problems*, especially for young *babies*. Nitrates prevent the *blood* from carrying *oxygen* properly and children can *turn blue* and even *die*.
3) To avoid these problems it's important that artificial nitrate fertilisers are applied *carefully* by all farmers — they must take care not to apply *too much*, and not if it's *going to rain* soon.

Higher Higher Higher

There's nowt wrong wi' just spreadin' muck on it...

Basically, this page is about how ammonia is turned into ammonium nitrate fertiliser. Alas there are some seriously tedious details which they seem to expect you to learn. Don't ask me why. Anyway, *the more you learn, the more you know*. (He said, wisely and meaninglessly.)

Transition Metals

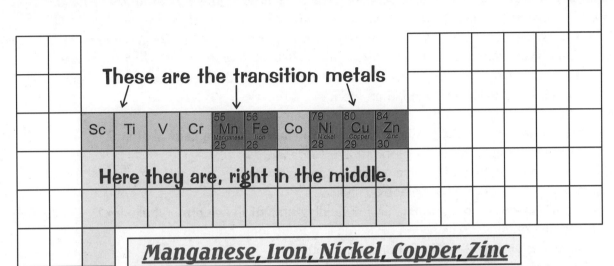

These are the transition metals

| | | | Sc | Ti | V | Cr | 55 Mn Manganese 25 | 56 Fe Iron 26 | Co | 79 Ni Nickel 28 | 80 Cu Copper 29 | 84 Zn Zinc 30 | | |

Here they are, right in the middle.

Manganese, Iron, Nickel, Copper, Zinc

You need to know the ones shown in red fairly well. If they wanted to be mean in the Exam *(if!)* they could cheerfully mention one of the others like scandium or cobalt or titanium or vanadium. Don't let it hassle you. They'll just be testing how well you can *"apply scientific knowledge to new information"*. In other words, just assume these "new" transition metals follow all the properties you've already learnt for the others. That's all it is, but it can really worry some folk.

Transition Metals *all have high melting point and high density*

They're *typical* metals. They have the properties you would expect of a proper metal:

1) *Good conductors* of heat and electricity.

2) Very *dense*, *strong* and *shiny*.

3) Iron melts at 1500°C, copper melts at 1100°C and zinc melts at 400°C.

Transition Metals *and their* compounds *all make good catalysts*

1) *Iron* is the catalyst used in the *Haber process* for making *ammonia*.

2) *Manganese (IV) oxide* is a good catalyst for the decomposition of *hydrogen peroxide*.

3) *Nickel* is useful for turning *oils into fats* for making margarine.

The compounds *are very colourful*

1) The compounds are colourful due to the *transition metal ion* they contain. e.g. Potassium chromate(VI) is *yellow*. Potassium manganate(VII) is *purple*. Copper (II) sulphate is *blue*.

2) The colour of people's *hair* (OK, maybe not this man's) and also the colours in *gemstones* like *blue sapphires* and *green emeralds* are all due to *transition metals*.

The transition metals *zinc* and *copper* make the alloy *brass* for trumpets and tubas.

...and Cast Iron is used to make Manhole Covers.

Apparently you should know that. So I'm told. Also don't forget that copper is used for electrical wiring and hot water pipes, and zinc is used to galvanise iron.

Lots of pretty colours — that's what we like to see...

There's quite a few things to learn about transition metals. First try to remember the headings. Then learn the details that go under each one. *Keep trying to scribble it all down.*

Revision Summary for Module Seven

Some more horrid questions to stress you out. The thing is though, why bother doing easy questions? These meaty monsters find out what you really know, and worse, what you really don't. Yeah, I know, it's kinda scary, but if you want to get anywhere in life you've got to face up to a bit of hardship. That's just the way it is. Take a few deep breaths and then try these:

1) Sketch an atom. Give five details about the nucleus and five details about the electrons.
2) What are the three particles found in an atom?
3) Draw a table showing their relative masses and charges.
4) How do the number of these particles compare to each other in a neutral atom?
5) What do the mass number and proton number represent?
6) Explain what an isotope is. (!) Give a well-known example.
7) List five facts (or "Rules") about electron shells.
8) Calculate the electron configuration and draw diagrams of the electron shells for Li, Ca, Ar & O.
9) What is ionic bonding? Which kind of atoms like to do ionic bonding?
10) Why do atoms want to form ionic bonds anyway?
11) Give three features of giant ionic structures.
12) What kind of ions are formed by elements in Groups I, II, and those in Groups VI and VII?
13) List the three main properties of ionic compounds.
14) Which atoms form 1+, 1-, 2+ and 2- ions?
15) Describe the electronic structure of the ions in these compounds: NaCl, MgO and $CaCl_2$.
16) What is covalent bonding?
17) Why do some atoms do covalent bonding instead of ionic bonding?
18) Describe and draw diagrams to illustrate the bonding in: H_2, HCl, NH_3, CH_4 and H_2O.
19) Draw simplified diagrams (not showing the electrons) of the five substances described above.
20) What are the two types of covalent substances? Give three examples of each type.
21) Give three physical properties for each of the two types of covalent substance.
22) Find A_r or M_r for these (use the periodic table inside the front cover):
      a) Ca   b) Ag   c) CO_2 d) $MgCO_3$ e) Na_2CO_3 f) ZnO   g) KOH   h) NH_3
23) What is the formula for calculating the percentage mass of an element in a compound?
      a) Calculate the percentage mass of carbon in   i) $CaCO_3$ ii) CO_2 iii) Methane
      b) Calculate the percentage mass of metal in these oxides: i) Na_2O ii) Fe_2O_3 iii) Al_2O_3
24) List the five steps of the method for finding an empirical formula (EF) from masses or %.
25) Work these out (using the periodic table):
      a) Find the EF for the iron oxide formed when 45.1g of iron reacts with 19.3g of oxygen.
      b) Find the EF for the compound formed when 227g of calcium reacts with 216g of fluorine.
26) Write down the three steps of the method for calculating reacting masses.
      a) What mass of magnesium oxide is produced when 112.1g of magnesium burns in air?
      b) What mass of sodium is needed to produce 108.2g of sodium oxide?
27) What mass of gas occupies 24 litres at room temperature and pressure?
28) Write down the formula for calculating the volume of a known mass of gas (at room T & P).
      a) What is the volume of 56.0g of nitrogen at room T & P?
      b) Find the volume of carbon dioxide produced when 5.6g of carbon is completely burned.
      c) What volume of oxygen will react with 25.0g of hydrogen to produce water?
29) What is a reversible reaction? Describe a simple reversible reaction involving solids.
30) Explain what is meant by dynamic equilibrium in a reversible reaction.
31) How does changing the temperature and pressure of a reaction alter the equilibrium?
32) How does this influence the choice of pressure for the Haber process?
33) What determines the choice of operating temperature for the Haber process?
34) List four properties of transition metals, and two properties of their compounds.
35) Name five transition metals, and give uses for two of them.

Magnetic Fields

There's a proper definition of a _magnetic field_ which you really ought to learn:

> A _MAGNETIC FIELD_ is a region where _MAGNETIC MATERIALS_ (like iron and steel) and also _WIRES CARRYING CURRENTS_ experience _A FORCE_ acting on them.

Learn All These Magnetic Field Diagrams, Arrow-Perfect

They're real likely to give you one of these diagrams to do in your Exam.
So make sure you know them, especially which way the _arrows point_ — _ALWAYS from N to S!_

Bar Magnet

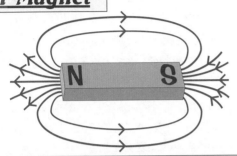

Solenoid

Same field as a bar magnet _outside_.

Strong and uniform field on the _inside_.

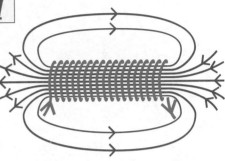

Two Bar Magnets Attracting

Opposite poles ATTRACT, as I'm sure you know.

Two Bar Magnets Repelling

Like poles REPEL, as you must surely know.

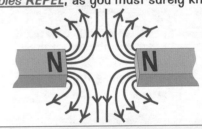

The Earth's Magnetic Field

Note that the _magnetic poles_ are _opposite_ to the _Geographic Poles_, i.e. the _south pole_ is at the _North Pole_ — if you see what I mean! That way the _north pole_ of a _compass needle_ points to it.

The Magnetic Field Round a Current-Carrying Wire

Current   Current

Magnetic Field

The Right Hand Thumb Rule shows which way the magnetic field goes

The Poles of a Solenoid

If you imagine looking directly into one end of a solenoid, the _direction of current flow_ tells you whether it's the _N or S pole_ you're looking at, as shown by the _two diagrams_ opposite. Make sure you remember those diagrams.

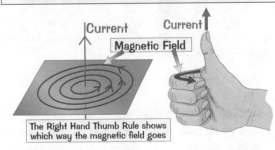

N-Pole   S-Pole

Magnetic fields — there's no getting away from them...

Mmm, this is a nice easy page for you isn't it. Learn the definition of what a magnetic field is and the six field diagrams. But pay loads of attention to what way the arrows are pointing — so many people lose marks on that. Once you think you know it, just _cover the page_ and _scribble_.

48

Electromagnets

Electromagnetic
Forces & Transformers

An Electromagnet Is Just a Coil of Wire with an Iron Core

1) _Electromagnets_ are simply a _solenoid_ (just a _coil of wire_) with a piece of _"soft" iron_ inside.
2) When _current flows_ through the _wires_ of the solenoid it creates a _magnetic field_ around it.
3) The _soft iron core_ has the effect of _increasing_ the _magnetic field strength_.
4) _"Soft"_ just means that it _doesn't retain its magnetism_, so that when the current is turned off, the _magnetism disappears_ with it. That means that you can turn the electromagnet _off_.

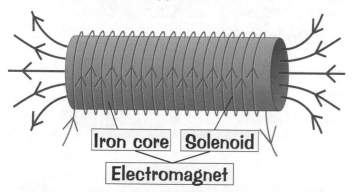

Iron core | Solenoid
Electromagnet

1) The _magnetic field_ around an _electromagnet_ is just like the one round a _bar magnet_, only _stronger_.
2) This means that the _ends_ of a _solenoid_ act like the _north pole_ and _south pole_ of a bar magnet.
3) Pretty obviously, if the direction of the _current_ is _reversed_, the N and S poles will _swap ends_.

The **STRENGTH** of an **ELECTROMAGNET** depends on **THREE FACTORS:**

1) The size of the **CURRENT**.
2) The number of **TURNS** the coil has.
3) What the **CORE** is made of.

Relay

E.g. A very big relay is used in _cars_ for switching the _starter motor_, because it draws a _very big current_.

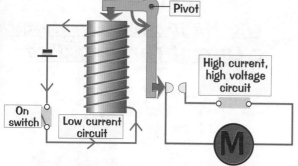

1) A _relay_ is a device which uses a _low current_ circuit to _switch_ a _high current_ circuit on/off.
2) When the switch in the low current circuit is _closed_ it turns the electromagnet _ON_ which _attracts_ the _iron rocker_.
3) The rocker _pivots_ and _closes_ the contacts in the high current circuit.
4) When the low current switch is _opened_, the electromagnet _stops_ pulling, the rocker returns, and the high current circuit is _broken_ again.

Electric Bell

These are used in schools to stress everyone out.

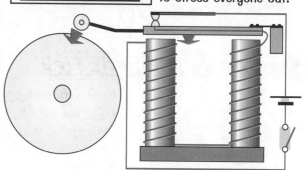

1) When the switch is _closed_, the electromagnets are turned _on_.
2) They pull the iron arm _DOWN_ which _clangs_ the bell, but at the same time _breaks_ the contact, which immediately _turns off_ the electromagnets.
3) The arm then _springs back_, which _closes_ the _contact_, and off we go again...
4) The whole sequence happens _very_ quickly, maybe _10 times a second_, so the bell sounds like a continuous _"brrriiiinnngg"_ sound. Nice.

Electromagnets really irritate me — I just get solenoid with them...

This is all very basic information, and really quite memorable I'd have thought. Learn the headings and diagrams first, then _cover the page_ and _scribble them down_. Then gradually fill in the other details. _Keep looking back and checking_. Try to learn _all_ the points. Lovely innit.

SEG Syllabus | Module Eight — Using Power

The Electric Motor

Anything carrying a _current_ in a _magnetic field_ will experience a _force_. There are _three important cases:_

A Current in a Magnetic Field Experiences a Force

The two tests below demonstrate the _force_ on a _current-carrying wire_ placed in a _magnetic field_. The _force_ gets _bigger_ if either the _current_ or the _magnetic field_ is made bigger.

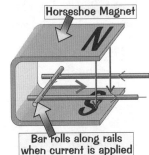

1) Note that in _both cases_ the _force_ on the wire is at _90°_ to both the _wire_ and to the _magnetic field_.
2) You can always _predict_ which way the _force_ will act using _Fleming's LHR_ as shown below.
3) To experience the _full force_, the _wire_ has to be at _90°_ to the _magnetic field_.
4) The _direction_ of the force is _reversed_ if either:
   a) the direction of the _current_ is reversed.
   b) the direction of the _magnetic field_ is reversed.

Horseshoe Magnet

Bar rolls along rails when current is applied

The Simple Electric Motor

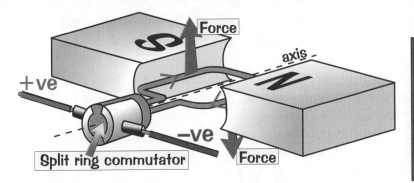

Force

axis

+ve

−ve

Force

Split ring commutator

4 Factors That Speed It Up

1) More _CURRENT_
2) More _TURNS_ on the coil
3) _STRONGER MAGNETIC FIELD_
4) A _SOFT IRON CORE_ in the coil

1) The diagram shows the _forces_ acting on the two _side arms_ of the _coil_.
2) These forces are just the _usual forces_ which act on _any current_ in a _magnetic field_.
3) Because the coil is on a _spindle_ and the forces act _one up_ and _one down_, it _rotates_.
4) The direction of the motor can be _reversed_ either by swapping the _polarity_ of the _DC supply_, or by swapping the _magnetic poles_ over.

Fleming's Left Hand Rule Tells You Which Way the Force Acts

1) They could test if you can do this, so _practise it_.
2) Using your _left hand_, point your _First finger_ in the direction of the _Field_ and your _seCond finger_ in the direction of the _Current_.
3) Your _thuMb_ will then point in the direction of the _force_ (Motion).

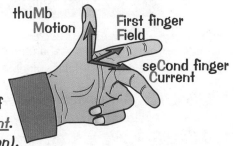

thuMb Motion

First finger Field

seCond finger Current

Fleming — how many broken wrists has he caused already...

Same old routine here. _Learn all the details_, diagrams and all, then _cover the page_ and _scribble it all down_ again _from memory_. I presume you do realise that you should be scribbling it down as scruffy as you like — because all you're trying to do is make sure that you really do _know it_.

Transformers

Transformers use *Electromagnetic Induction*. So they will *only* work on *AC*.

Transformers Change the Voltage — but Only AC Voltages

They are used in the production and distribution of our mains electricity, and there's two types:
1) *Step-up* transformers step the voltage *up*. They have *more turns* on the secondary coil.
2) *Step-down* transformers step the voltage *down*. They have *fewer turns* on the secondary.
They drop the voltage from 400,000V to a "safe" 230V for our homes.

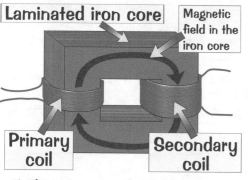
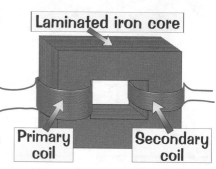

1) The *laminated iron core* is purely for transferring the *magnetic field* from the primary coil to the secondary.
2) The iron core is *laminated* with layers of *insulation* to reduce the *eddy currents* which *heat it up*, and therefore *waste energy*.

1) The primary coil produces *a magnetic field* which stays within the *iron core* and this means it *all* passes through the *secondary* coil.
2) Because there is *alternating current* (AC) in the *primary* coil, this means that the magnetic field in the iron core is *reversing* (50 times a second, usually) — i.e. it's a *changing* field.
3) This rapidly *changing* magnetic field is then experienced by the *secondary coil* and this *induces* an *alternating voltage* in it — *electromagnetic induction* of a voltage in fact.
4) The *relative number of turns* on the two coils determines whether the voltage created in the secondary is *greater* or *less* than the voltage in the primary.
5) If you supplied DC to the primary, you'd get *NOTHING* out of the secondary at all. Sure, there'd still be a field in the iron core, but it wouldn't be *constantly changing*, so there'd be no *induction* in the secondary because you need a *changing field* to induce a voltage. Don't you! So don't forget it — transformers only work with *AC*. They won't work with DC *at all*.

The Transformer Equation — Use It Either Way Up

In words: The *RATIO OF TURNS* on the two coils equals the *RATIO OF THEIR VOLTAGES*.

$$\frac{\text{Primary Voltage}}{\text{Secondary Voltage}} = \frac{\text{Number of turns on Primary}}{\text{Number of turns on Secondary}}$$

$$\frac{V_P}{V_S} = \frac{N_P}{N_S} \quad \text{or} \quad \frac{V_S}{V_P} = \frac{N_S}{N_P}$$

Well, it's *just another formula*. You stick in the numbers *you've got* and work out the one *that's left*. It's real useful to remember you can write it *either way up* — this example's much trickier algebra-wise if you start with V_S on the bottom...

EXAMPLE: A transformer has 40 turns on the primary and 800 on the secondary. If the input voltage is 1,000V find the output voltage.
ANSWER: $V_S/V_P = N_S/N_P$ so $V_S/1,000 = 800/40$ $V_S = 1,000 \times (800/40) = \underline{20,000V}$

The ubiquitous iron core — where would we be without it...

Besides their iron core, transformers have lots of other *important* details which also need to be *learnt*. You'll need practise with that tricky equation too. It's unusual because it can't be put into formula triangles, but other than that the method is the same. Just *practise*.

The National Grid

1) The *National Grid* is the *network* of pylons and cables which *covers* the whole of Britain.
2) It takes electricity from the *power stations*, to just where it's needed in *homes* and *industry*.
3) It enables power to be *generated* anywhere on the grid, and to then be *supplied* anywhere else on the grid.

All Power Stations Are Pretty Much the Same

They all have a *boiler* of some sort that makes *steam*, which drives a *turbine*, which drives a *generator*. The generator produces *electricity* (by *induction*) by *rotating* an *electromagnet* within coils of wire (see Module 4).

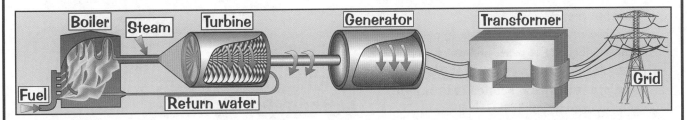

Learn all these features of the *NATIONAL GRID* — power stations, transformers, pylons, etc:

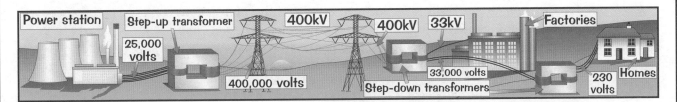

Pylon Cables Are at 400,000 V to Keep the Current Low

You need to understand why the *VOLTAGE* is so *HIGH* and why it's *AC*. Learn these points:

1) The formula for *power supplied* is: *Power = Voltage × Current* or: $P = V \times I$.
2) So to transmit a *lot* of power, you either need high *voltage* or high *current*.
3) The problem with *high current* is the *loss* (as heat) due to the *resistance* of the cables.
4) The formula for *heat loss* due to resistance in the cables is: $P = I^2R$.
5) Because of the I^2 bit, if the current is *10 times* bigger, the losses will be *100 times* bigger.
6) So it's much *cheaper* to boost the voltage up to *400,000V* and keep the current *very low*.
7) This requires *transformers* as well as *big* pylons with *huge* insulators, but it's still *cheaper*.
8) The transformers have to *step* the voltage *up* at one end, for *efficient* transmission, and then bring it back down to *safe* useable levels at the other end.
9) This is why it has to be *AC* on the National Grid — so that the *transformers* will work!

You can also reduce the heat loss by increasing the thickness of the cable (which reduces the resistance). But thicker cable costs more, so a compromise has to be made.

400,000 volts? — that could give you a bit of a buzz...

Quite a few tricky details on this page. The power station and National Grid are easy enough, but fully explaining why pylon cables are at 400,000V is a bit trickier — but you do need to learn it. When you watch TV think of the route the electricity has to travel. *Scribble it down.*

Static Electricity

Static electricity is all about charges that are _NOT_ free to move. This causes them to build up in one place and it often ends with a _spark_ or a _shock_ when they do finally move.

1) Build-Up of Static Is Caused by Friction

1) When two _insulating_ materials are _rubbed_ together, electrons will be _scraped off one_ and _dumped_ on the other.
2) This'll leave a _positive_ static charge on one and a _negative_ static charge on the other.
3) _Which way_ the electrons are transferred _depends_ on the _two materials_ involved.
4) Electrically charged objects _attract_ small objects placed near them.
   (Try this: rub a balloon on a woolly pully – then put it near tiddly bits of paper and watch them jump.)
5) The classic examples are _polythene_ and _acetate_ rods being rubbed with a _cloth duster_, as shown in the diagrams:

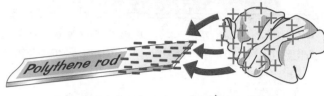

With the _polythene rod_, electrons move _from the duster_ to the rod.

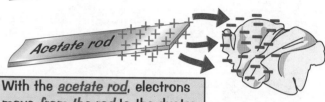

With the _acetate rod_, electrons move _from the rod_ to the duster.

2) Only Electrons Move — Never the Positive Charges

Watch out for this in Exams. Both +ve and –ve electrostatic charges are only ever produced by the movement of _electrons_. The positive charges _definitely do not move!_ A positive static charge is always caused by electrons _moving_ away elsewhere, as shown above. Don't forget!

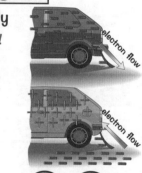

A charged conductor can be _discharged safely_ by connecting it to earth with a _metal strap_. The electrons flow _down_ the strap to the ground if the charge is _negative_ and flow _up_ the strap from the ground if the charge is _positive_.

3) Like Charges Repel, Opposite Charges Attract

This is _easy_ and, I'd have thought, _kind of obvious_.
Two things with _opposite_ electric charges are _attracted_ to each other.
Two things with the _same_ electric charge will _repel_ each other.
These forces get _weaker_ the _further apart_ the two things are.

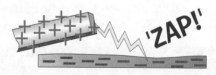

4) Sparks Are Caused by Unbalanced Charges

The greater the _CHARGE_ on an _isolated_ object, the greater the _VOLTAGE_ between it and the earth. If the voltage gets _big enough_ there's a _spark_ which _jumps_ across the gap. High voltage cables can be _dangerous_ for this reason. Big sparks have been known to _leap_ from _overhead cables_ to earth. But not often.

'ZAP!'

Phew — it's enough to make your hair stand on end...

The way to tackle this page is to first _learn the four headings_ till you can _scribble them all down_. Then learn all the details, and keep practising by _covering the page_ and scribbling down the headings with as many details as you can remember for each one. Just _keep trying_...

Static Electricity

They like asking you to give _quite detailed examples_ in Exams. Make sure you _learn all these details_.

Static Electricity Being Helpful:

Dust Removal in Chimneys:

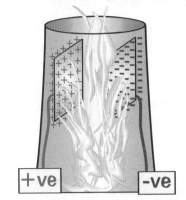

+ve   -ve

1) Just put a set of _charged plates_ in a _chimney_ or extractor duct and the particles of smoke or dust will be _attracted_ to them.
2) Every now and then you _turn off_ the electricity and _shake the dust into a bag_ — easy peasy. These are known as _electrostatic smoke precipitators_.

Static Electricity Being a Little Joker:

Clothing Crackles

When _synthetic clothes_ are _dragged_ over each other (like in a _tumble drier_) or over your _head_, electrons get scraped off, leaving _unbalanced charges_ between the parts, and that leads to the inevitable: — _forces of attraction_ (i.e. they stick together) and little _sparks/shocks_ as the charges _rearrange themselves_.

Static Electricity Playing at Terrorist:

1) Lightning

Rain droplets fall to Earth with _positive charge_. This creates a _huge charge inbalance_ and a _big spark_.

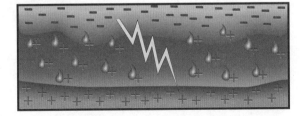

2) The Old Fuel-Filling Nightmare:

1) As _fuel_ flows out of a _filler pipe_, static charge can _build up_.
2) This can easily lead to a _SPARK_, which can ignite the fuel vapour and — _BOOM!_
3) _The solution_: make the nozzles out of _METAL_ so that the charge is _conducted away_, instead of building up.
4) It's also good to have _earthing straps_ between the _fuel tank_ and the _fuel pipe_.

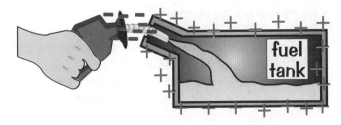

fuel tank

Static electricity — learn the shocking truth...

This page is nicely broken up into three main sections, which makes it quite a bit easier to learn. First learn the main headings, then the subheadings, and then all the details that go with each. Slowly you _build it all up_ in your head till you can _scribble it all down_.

Electric Charge

Current Is Just the Flow of Charges

CURRENT flows any time _charge moves from one place to another_. Of course with a _spark_ it doesn't last very long. But join up a few bits of wire in a loop and you've got a _circuit_. Give it a _power supply_ — like a _battery_ — and current can flow _continually_ (...well, until your battery runs out).

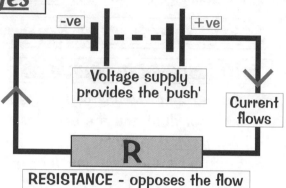

Voltage supply provides the 'push'

Current flows

R

RESISTANCE - opposes the flow

Charges Are Normally Electrons, but...

If the current is flowing through a **SOLUTION**, the charges are dissolved _IONS_.

Charge Is Measured in Coulombs — Given by the Formula "Q=It"

When _current_ (I) flows past a point in a circuit for a length of _time_ (t) then _charge_ (Q) has passed. This is given by the formula: $Q = It$
More charge passes around the circuit when a _bigger current_ flows.

EXAMPLE: A charge of 15 coulombs flows past a point in 3 seconds. What is the current?
ANSWER: $I = Q/t = 15/3 = 5A$.

Voltage and Energy Change

1) When electrical _charge_ (Q) goes through a _change_ in voltage (V), then _energy_ (E) is _transferred_.
Energy is _supplied_ to the charge at the _power source_ to raise it through a voltage.
The charge _gives up_ this energy when it _falls_ through any _voltage drop_ in _components_ elsewhere in the circuit.
The formula is real simple: $E = QV$

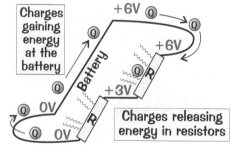

Charges gaining energy at the battery

+6V

+6V

+3V

0V

0V

Charges releasing energy in resistors

2) The _bigger_ the _change_ in voltage, the _more energy_ is transferred for a _given amount of charge_ passing through the circuit. That means that a battery with a _bigger voltage_ will supply _more energy_ to the circuit for every _coulomb_ of charge that flows round it, because the charge is raised up _"higher"_ at the start (see above diagram) — and as the diagram shows, _more energy_ will be _dissipated_ in the circuit too.

Electrical Power

1) _Electrical Power_ is defined as the _rate of transfer of electrical energy_. It is measured in _watts_ (W), which is just _joules per second_ (J/s).
2) The standard formula for _electrical power_ is: $P=VI$
3) If you _combine_ it with $V=I \times R$ by replacing the "V" with "I×R", you get: $P=I^2R$
4) If instead you use V=I×R and replace the "I" with "V/R", you get: $P=V^2/R$
5) You _choose_ which _one_ of these formulae to use, purely and simply by seeing which one contains the _three quantities_ that are _involved_ in the problem you're looking at.

Electricity — why does it all turn out so dreary...

I try to make it interesting, really I do. I mean, underneath it all, electricity is pretty good stuff, but somehow every page just seems to end up stuffed full of interminably dreary facts. Well look, _I tried_, OK. It may be dreary but you've just gotta _learn it all_, and that's that.

Work Done, Energy and Power

When a *force* moves an *object*, *ENERGY IS TRANSFERRED* and *WORK IS DONE*.

That statement sounds far more complicated than it needs to. Try this:

1) Whenever something *moves*, something else is providing some sort of *"effort"* to move it.
2) The thing putting the *effort* in needs a *supply* of energy (like *fuel* or *food* or *electricity*, etc.)
3) It then does *"work"* by *moving* the object — and one way or another it *transfers* the energy it receives (as fuel) into *other forms*.
4) Whether this energy is transferred *"usefully"* (e.g. by *lifting a load*) or is *"wasted"* (e.g. lost as *friction*), you can still say that *"work is done"*. Just like Batman and Bruce Wayne, *"work done"* and *"energy transferred"* are indeed *"one and the same"*. (And they're both in *joules*).

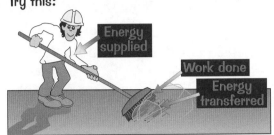

It's Just Another Trivial Formula:

Work Done = Force × Distance

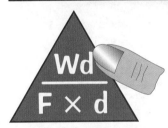

Wd / F × d

Whether the force is *friction* or *weight* or *tension in a rope*, it's always the same. To find how much *energy* has been *transferred* (in joules), you just multiply the force in N by the *distance moved in m*. Easy as that. I'll show you...

EXAMPLE: Some hooligan kids drag an old tractor tyre 5m over rough ground. They pull with a total force of 340N. Find the energy transferred.
ANSWER: Wd = F×d = 340 × 5 = 1,700J. Phew — easy peasy isn't it?

Power Is the "Rate of Doing Work" — i.e. How Much Per Second

POWER is *not* the same thing as *force*, nor *energy*. A *powerful* machine is not necessarily one that can exert a strong *force* (though it usually ends up that way).
A *POWERFUL* machine is one that transfers *A LOT OF ENERGY IN A SHORT SPACE OF TIME*. This is the *very easy formula* for power:

$$\text{Power} = \frac{\text{Work done}}{\text{Time taken}}$$

EXAMPLE: A motor transfers 4.8kJ of useful energy in 2 minutes. Find its power output.
ANSWER: P = Wd / t = 4,800/120 = 40W (or 40 J/s)
(Note that the kJ had to be turned into J, and the minutes into seconds.)

Wd / P × t

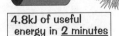

4.8kJ of useful energy in 2 minutes

Power Is Measured in Watts (or J/s)

The proper unit of power is the *watt*. *One watt = 1 joule of energy transferred per second*. *Power* means "how much energy *per second*", so *watts* are the same as *"joules per second"* (J/s). Don't ever say "watts per second" — it's *nonsense*.

Revise work done — what else...

"Energy transferred" and *"work done"* are the same thing. I wonder how many times I need to say that before you'll remember. Power is *"work done divided by time taken"*. I wonder how many times you've got to see that before you realise you're supposed to *learn it* as well...

Kinetic and Potential Energy

Kinetic Energy Is Energy of Movement

1) Anything that is _moving_ has _kinetic energy_.

2 The _kinetic energy_ of something depends both on its _MASS_ and _SPEED_.

3) The _more_ it weighs and the _faster_ it's going, the _greater_ its kinetic energy will be.

4) That's why the _stopping distance_ for a _fast car_ is much _greater_ than that for a _slow car_ — the faster car has to lose far more kinetic energy before it comes to a halt.

There's a _slightly tricky_ formula for it, so you have to concentrate _a little bit harder_ for this one. But hey, that's life — it can be real tough sometimes:

$$\text{Kinetic Energy} = \tfrac{1}{2} \times \text{mass} \times \text{velocity}^2$$

EXAMPLE: A car of mass 2,450kg is travelling at 38m/s. Calculate its kinetic energy.

ANSWER: It's pretty easy. You just plug the numbers into the formula — but watch the "v^2"! $KE = \tfrac{1}{2} m v^2 = \tfrac{1}{2} \times 2450 \times 38^2 = \underline{1,768,900J}$ (_joules_ because it's _energy_)

(When the car stops suddenly, all this energy is dissipated as heat at the brakes — it's a lot of heat)

K.E. $\dfrac{}{\tfrac{1}{2} \times m \times v^2}$

small mass, not fast low kinetic energy

big fast lorries Ltd

big mass, real fast high kinetic energy

Elastic Potential Energy Is Energy Stored in Springs

Elastic potential energy is the energy _stored_ when _work is done on an object_ to distort it. If a spring is either _compressed or stretched_, then it is said to have _elastic potential energy_.

Gravitational Potential Energy Is Energy Due to Height

Gravitational potential energy is the energy _stored in an object_ because it has been raised to a specific height _against_ the force of gravity.

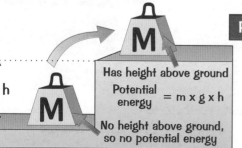

Has height above ground Potential energy = m x g x h

No height above ground, so no potential energy

$$\text{Potential Energy} = \text{mass} \times g \times \text{height}$$

Quite often _gravitational potential energy_ is just called _"potential energy"_, but you should really use its full name. The proper name for g is _"gravitational field strength"_. _On Earth_ this has the value of $\underline{g = 10m/s^2}$ (N/kg).

P.E. $\dfrac{}{m \times g \times h}$

Kinetic energy — just get a move on and learn it, OK...

Phew! A couple of tricky formulae here. I mean gosh they've got more than three letters in them. Still, at least they fit into formula triangles, so you may still have some small chance of getting them right. Come on, I'm joking. Formulae are always _a doddle_, aren't they?

Higher Higher Higher

K.E. and P.E. — Some Examples

1) Working Out Potential Energy

EXAMPLE: A sheep of mass 47kg is slowly raised through 6.3m. Find the gain in potential energy.

ANSWER: This is pretty easy.
You just plug the numbers into the formula:
$PE = mgh = 47 \times 10 \times 6.3 = \underline{2,961J}$
(joules again because it's energy again.)

2) Calculating Your Power Output

Both cases use the same formula:

$$\text{POWER} = \frac{\text{ENERGY TRANSFERRED}}{\text{TIME TAKEN}} \quad \text{or} \quad P = \frac{E}{t}$$

a) The Timed Run Upstairs:

In this case the *"energy transferred"* is simply the *potential energy you gain* (= mgh).
Hence $POWER = mgh/t$

Power output
= En. transferred/time
= mgh/t
= $(62 \times 10 \times 12) \div 14$
= $\underline{531W}$

b) The Timed Acceleration:

This time the *energy transferred* is the *kinetic energy you gain* (= $\frac{1}{2}mv^2$).
Hence $POWER = \frac{1}{2}mv^2/t$

Power output
= En. transferred/time
= $\frac{1}{2}mv^2/t$
= $(\frac{1}{2} \times 62 \times 8^2) \div 4$
= $\underline{496W}$

3) Calculating the Speed of Falling Objects

When something falls, its *potential energy* is *converted* into *kinetic energy*.
Hence the *further* it falls, the *faster* it goes.
In practice, some of the PE will be *dissipated* as *heat* due to *air resistance*, but in Exam questions they'll likely say you can *ignore* air resistance, in which case you'll just need to remember this *simple* and *really quite obvious formula*:

Kinetic energy *GAINED* = Potential Energy *LOST*

EXAMPLE: A mouldy tomato of mass 140g is dropped from a height of 1.7m. Calculate its speed as it hits the floor.

ANSWER: There are four key steps to this method — and you've gotta learn them:

Step 1) Find the PE lost: = mgh = $0.14 \times 10 \times 1.7 = \underline{2.38J}$. This must also be the KE gained.

Step 2) Equate the number of joules of KE gained to the KE formula with v in, " $\frac{1}{2}mv^2$ ":
$$2.38 = \frac{1}{2}mv^2$$

Step 3) Stick the numbers in: $2.38 = \frac{1}{2} \times 0.14 \times v^2$ or $2.38 = 0.07 \times v^2$
$2.38 \div 0.07 = v^2$ so $v^2 = 34$

Step 4) Square root: $v = \sqrt{34} = \underline{5.83 \text{ m/s}}$
Easy peasy? Not really no, but if you practise learning the four steps you'll find it's not too bad.

Revise falling objects — just don't lose your grip...

This is it. This is the zenith of GCSE Physics. This is the nearest it gets to *real* Physics (A-level). Look at that terrifying square root sign for a start — and a four step method. Scary stuff.

58

Forces and Acceleration

Force, Acceleration
& Pressure

Speed and Velocity Are Both Just: HOW FAST YOU'RE GOING

Speed and velocity are both measured in _m/s_ (or km/h or mph). They both simply say _how fast_ you're going, but there's a _subtle difference_ between them that _you need to know_:

SPEED is just _HOW FAST_ you're going (e.g. 30mph or 20m/s) with no regard to the direction.
VELOCITY however must _ALSO_ have the _DIRECTION_ specified, e.g. 30mph _north_ or 20m/s, 060°

A _force_ is simply a _push_ or a _pull_. There are only _six_ different forces for you to know about:

> 1) _GRAVITY_ or _WEIGHT_ always acting straight _downwards_.
> 2) _REACTION FORCE_ from a _surface_, usually acting _straight upwards_.
> 3) _THRUST_ or _PUSH_ or _PULL_ due to an engine or rocket _speeding something up_.
> 4) _DRAG_ or _AIR RESISTANCE_ or _FRICTION_ which is _slowing the thing down_.
> 5) _LIFT_ due to an _aeroplane wing_.
> 6) _TENSION_ in a _rope_ or _cable_.

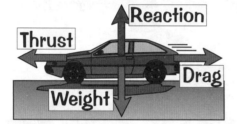 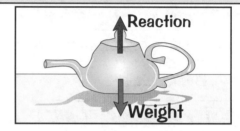

All Forces Are Measured in Newtons

That's _newtons_ with symbol _N_. i.e. the _force_ of gravity on an object of _1kg_ will be _10N_.

Acceleration Is How Quickly You're Speeding Up

Acceleration is definitely _NOT_ the same as _velocity_ or _speed_.

Every time you read or write the word _acceleration_, remind yourself: "_acceleration_ is _COMPLETELY DIFFERENT_ from _velocity_. Acceleration is how _quickly_ the velocity is _changing_."

Velocity is a simple idea. Acceleration is altogether more _subtle_, which is why it's _confusing_.

Acceleration — the Formula:

$$\text{Acceleration} = \frac{\text{Change in Velocity}}{\text{Time Taken}}$$

Well, it's _just another formula_. Just like all the others. Three things in a _formula triangle_. Mind you, there are _two_ tricky things with this one. First there's the "ΔV", which means working out the "_change in velocity_", as shown in the example below, rather than just putting a _simple value_ for speed or velocity in. Secondly there's the _units_ of acceleration which are m/s². _Not m/s_, which is _velocity_, but m/s². Got it? No? Let's try once more: _Not m/s_, _but m/s²_.

EXAMPLE: A skulking cat accelerates from 2m/s to 6m/s in 5.6s. Find its acceleration.
ANSWER: Using the formula triangle: a = ΔV/t = (6 - 2) / 5.6 = 4 ÷ 5.6 = _0.71 m/s²_
All pretty basic stuff I'd say.

Velocity and acceleration — learn the difference...

It's true — some people don't realise that velocity and acceleration are totally different things. Hard to believe I know — all part of the great mystery and tragedy of life I suppose. Anyway. Learn the definitions and the formulae, _cover the page_ and _scribble it all down again_.

Higher Higher Higher (left margin)
Higher Higher Higher (right margin)

Laws of Motion

Around about the time of the Great Plague in the 1660s, a chap called _Isaac Newton_ worked out the _Three Laws of Motion_. At first they might seem kind of obscure or irrelevant, but to be perfectly blunt, if you can't understand these _three simple laws_ then you'll never fully understand _forces and motion_:

First Law — Balanced Forces Mean No Change in Velocity

So long as the forces on an object are all _BALANCED_, then it'll just _STAY STILL_, or else if it's already moving it'll just carry on at the _SAME VELOCITY_ — so long as the forces are all _BALANCED_.

1) When a train or car or bus or anything else is _moving_ at a _constant velocity_ then the _forces_ on it must all be _BALANCED_.

2) Never let yourself entertain the _ridiculous idea_ that things need a constant overall force to _keep_ them moving — NO NO NO NO NO NO!

3) To keep going at a _steady speed_, there must be _ZERO RESULTANT FORCE_ — and don't you forget it.

Second Law — A Resultant Force Means Acceleration

If there is an _UNBALANCED FORCE_, then the object will _ACCELERATE_ in that direction.

1) An _unbalanced_ force will always produce _acceleration_ (or deceleration).

2) This _"acceleration"_ can take _FIVE_ different forms:
Starting, _stopping_, _speeding up_, _slowing down_, and _changing direction_.

3) On a force diagram, the _arrows_ will be _unequal_:

Don't ever say: "If something's moving there must be an overall resultant force acting on it".

Not so. If there's an _overall_ force it will always _accelerate_. You get _steady_ speed from _balanced_ forces. I wonder how many times I need to say that same thing before you remember it?

Three Points That Should Be Obvious:

1) The bigger the _force_, the _GREATER_ the _acceleration_ or _deceleration_.

2) The bigger the _mass_, the _SMALLER_ the _acceleration_.

3) To get a _big_ mass to accelerate _as fast_ as a _small_ mass, it needs a _bigger_ force.
Just think about pushing _heavy_ trolleys and it should all seem _fairly obvious_, I would hope.

Laws of motion? Repeal them at once — it's an outrage...

There's quite a few points on this page, and you really need to know them all — those laws of motion are pretty fundamental stuff. Just take each of the laws at a time, read through the points, _cover them up_, and try to _reproduce them_. Perfect material for _mini-essays_, I'd say.

Resultant Forces

The Overall Unbalanced Force Is Often Called the Resultant Force

Any _resultant force_ will produce _acceleration_, and this is the _formula_ for it:

$$\textsf{F = ma} \quad \text{or} \quad \textsf{a = F/m}$$

m = mass, a = acceleration, F is always the _RESULTANT FORCE_.

Resultant Force Is Real Important — Especially for "F = ma"

The notion of _RESULTANT FORCE_ is a real important one for you to get your head round. It's not especially tricky, it's just that it seems to get kind of _ignored_.

In most _real_ situations there are at least _two forces_ acting on an object along any direction. The _overall_ effect of these forces will decide the _motion_ of the object — whether it will _accelerate_, _decelerate_, or stay at a _steady speed_. The _"overall effect"_ is found by just _adding or subtracting_ the forces which point along the _same_ direction. The overall force you get is called the _RESULTANT FORCE_.

And when you use the _formula "F = ma"_,   F must always be the _RESULTANT FORCE_.

Example 1

_Q._   _What force is needed to accelerate a mass of 12kg at 5m/s² ?_
ANS. The question is asking for _force_
         — so you need a formula with _"F = something-or-other"_.
Since they also give you values for _mass_ and _acceleration_, the
formula _"F = ma"_ really should be a _pretty obvious choice_, surely.
So just _stick_ in the numbers they give you where the letters are:
_m = 12_, _a = 5_, so _"F = ma"_ gives F = 12 × 5 = _60N_
(It's _newtons_ because force always is).
(Notice that you don't really need to _fully understand_ what's going on — you
just need to know _how to use formulae_).

Example 2

EXAMPLE: _A car of mass of 1,750kg has an engine which provides a driving force of 5,200N._
            At 70mph the drag force acting on the car is 5,150N.
            Find its acceleration a) when first setting off from rest b) at 70mph.

ANSWER: 1) First draw a force diagram for both cases (no need to show the vertical forces):

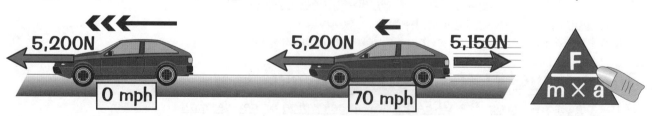

2) Work out the resultant force in each case, and apply "F = ma" using the formula triangle:

Resultant force = 5,200N	Resultant force = 5,200 – 5,150 = 50N
a = F/m = 5,200 ÷ 1,750 = <u>3.0 m/s²</u>	a = F/m = 50 ÷ 1750 = <u>0.03 m/s²</u>

Hey, did you know — an unbalanced force causes ac...

Make sure you fully understand what's happening in each of the calculations above. As with all calculations, the key to the stuff on this page is _practice_. There's simply _no substitute_...

Reaction Forces and Friction

The Third Law — Reaction Forces

If object A *EXERTS A FORCE* on object B, then object B exerts *THE EXACT OPPOSITE FORCE* on object A.

1) That means if you *push* against a wall, the wall will *push back* against you, *just as hard*.
2) And as soon as you *stop* pushing, *so does the wall*. Kinda clever really.
3) If you think about it, there must be an *opposing force* when you lean against a wall — otherwise you (and the wall) would *fall over*.
4) If you *pull* a cart, whatever force *you exert* on the rope, the rope exerts on *you*.
5) If you put a book on a table, the *weight* of the book acts *downwards* on the table — and the table exerts an *equal and opposite* force *upwards* on the book.
6) If you support a book on your *hand*, the book exerts its *weight* downwards on you, and you provide an *upwards* force on the book and it all stays nicely *in balance*.

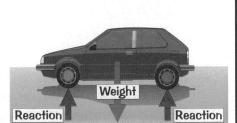

In *Exam* questions they may well *test* this by getting you to fill in some *extra arrow* to represent the *reaction force*. Learn this *very important fact*:

Whenever an object is on a horizontal *SURFACE*, there'll always be a *REACTION FORCE* pushing *UPWARDS*, supporting the object. The total *REACTION FORCE* will be *EQUAL AND OPPOSITE* to the weight.

Friction Is Always There to Slow Things Down

1) If an object has *no force* propelling it along it will always *slow down and stop* because of *friction*.
2) Friction always acts in the *opposite* direction to movement.
3) To travel at a *steady* speed, the driving force needs to *balance* the frictional forces.

Two Examples You Need to Know:

1) Friction between *solid surfaces* that are *gripping*. Acting between the a *tyre* and the *road*, this is the force that allows a car to corner (pretty handy, really).
2) *Air resistance*. This *increases as the speed increases* — so a faster car will have to do more work to accelerate a given amount. And the final speed of a falling object will depend on its air resistance (so *parachutes* are designed to have a *very high* air resistance).

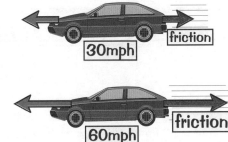
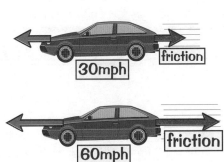

Learning about air resistance — it can be a real drag...

It looks like mini-essay time to me. There's a lot of details swirling around here, so definitely the best way of checking how much you know is to *scribble down a mini-essay* for each of the sections. Then *check back* and see what you *missed*. Then try again. *And keep trying*.

Stopping Distances for Cars

They're pretty keen on this for Exam questions, so make sure you *learn it properly*.

The Many Factors That Affect Your Total Stopping Distance

The distance it takes to stop a car is divided into the *THINKING DISTANCE* and the *BRAKING DISTANCE*.

1) Thinking Distance

"The distance the car travels in the split-second between a hazard appearing and the driver applying the brakes".

It's affected by *THREE MAIN FACTORS*:

a) *How FAST you're going* — obviously. Whatever your reaction time, the *faster* you're going, the *further* you'll go.

b) *How DOPEY you are* — This is affected by *tiredness*, *drugs*, *alcohol*, *old-age*, and a *careless* blasé attitude.

c) *How BAD the VISIBILITY is* — lashing rain and oncoming lights, etc. make *hazards* harder to spot.

The figures below for typical stopping distances are from the Highway code. It's frightening to see just how far it takes to stop when you're going at 70mph.

2) Braking Distance

"The distance the car travels during its deceleration whilst the brakes are being applied."

It's affected by *FOUR MAIN FACTORS*:

a) *How FAST you're going* — obviously. The *faster* you're going, the *further* it takes to stop (see below).

b) *How HEAVILY LOADED the vehicle is* — with the *same* brakes, *a heavily-laden* vehicle takes *longer to stop*. A car won't stop as quick when it's full of people and luggage and towing a caravan.

c) *How good your BRAKES are* — all brakes must be checked and maintained *regularly*. Worn or faulty brakes will let you down *catastrophically* just when you need them the *most*, i.e. in an *emergency*.

d) *How good the GRIP is* — this depends on *THREE THINGS*:
   1) *road surface*, 2) *weather* conditions, 3) *tyres*.

30 mph	50 mph	70 mph
9m	15m	21m
14m		
6 car lengths	38m	
	13 car lengths	75m
		24 car lengths

Thinking distance

Braking distance

Leaves and diesel spills and muck on t'road are *serious hazards* because they're *unexpected*. *Wet* or *icy roads* are always much more *slippy* than dry roads, but often you only discover this when you try to *brake* hard! Tyres should have a minimum *tread depth* of *1.6mm*. This is essential for getting rid of the *water* in wet conditions. Without *tread*, a tyre will simply *ride* on a *layer of water* and skid *very easily*. This is called "*aquaplaning*" and isn't nearly as cool as it sounds.

Stopping Distances Increase Alarmingly with Extra Speed

— Mainly Because of the v^2 Bit in KE=½mv^2

To stop a car, the *kinetic energy*, ½mv^2, has to be *converted to heat energy* at the *brakes and tyres*: If you *double the speed*, you double the value of *v*, but the v^2 means that the *KE* is then increased by a factor of *four*. This means that you need *4 times* the *distance* to stop when applying the *maximum* possible braking force.

Muck on t'road, eh — by gum, it's grim up North...

They mention this specifically in the syllabus and are very likely to test you on it since it involves safety. Learn all the details and write yourself a *mini-essay* to see how much you *really know*.

Higher Higher

Pressure on Surfaces

Pressure Is Not the Same as Force

Too many people get _force_ and _pressure_ mixed up — but there's a _pretty serious difference_ between them.

> _PRESSURE_ is defined as the _FORCE ACTING_ on _UNIT AREA_ of a surface.

Now read on, learn, and squirm with pleasure as another great mystery of the Physical Universe is exposed to your numb and weary mind...

Force Vs Pressure Has a Lot to Do with Damaging Surfaces

A force concentrated in a _small area_ creates a _high pressure_ — which means that the thing will _sink_ into the surface. But with a _big_ area, you get a _low_ pressure which means it _doesn't_ sink into the surface.

A Force Spread over a Big Area Means Low Pressure and No Sinking

Foundations   Snow shoes and skis   Tractor tyres   Drawing pins

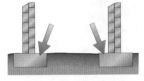 

A Force Concentrated on a Small Area Means High Pressure and Damage

Ice skates   Stiletto heels   Sharp knives   Drawing pins

Pressure in Liquids Acts in All Directions and Increases with Depth

1) In a _gas_ or _liquid_ the same pressure acts outwards in _all_ directions. This is _different_ from solids, which transmit forces in _one direction only_.
2) Also, the _pressure_ in a liquid or gas _increases_ as you go _deeper_. This is due to the _weight_ of all the stuff _above it_ pushing down. Imagine the weight of all the water _directly_ over you at a depth of 100m. All of that is _pushing down_ on the water below and _increasing the pressure_ down there. This is what _limits_ the depth that submarines can reach before the pressure _crushes_ the hull or bursts through a weak join somewhere.
3) The _increase_ in pressure also depends on the _density_ of the fluid. Air is _not very dense_, so air pressure changes _relatively little_ as you go up through the atmosphere. Water _is_ pretty dense though, so the pressure increases very quickly as you go _deeper_.

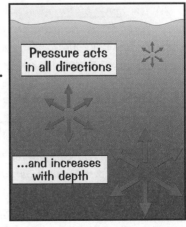

Pressure acts in all directions

...and increases with depth

Spread the load and reduce the pressure — start revising now...

It's funny old stuff is pressure. Force is a nice easy concept and people usually do fine with it. But pressure is just that bit trickier — and that means it can cause people a lot of gyp. Make sure you _learn all these details_ about pressure. They're all worth marks in the Exam.

Pressure = Force / Area

$$\text{Pressure} = \frac{\text{Force}}{\text{Area}}$$

The normal _unit of pressure_ is the _pascal_, Pa, which is the same as N/m². There is a fancy definition of the pascal. If you think it helps, you can learn it:

> A pressure of __ONE PASCAL__ is exerted by a __FORCE OF 1N__ acting at right angles to an __AREA of 1m²__

They may well give you questions with areas given in _cm²_. Don't try to _convert cm² to m²_, which is a bit tricky. Instead, just work out the pressure using P = F/A in the normal way, but give the answer as N/cm² rather than N/m² (Pa). Do remember that _N/cm²_ is _not_ the same as pascals (which are N/m²).

Hydraulics — the Main Application of "P = F/A"

Hydraulic systems all use _two important features_ of _pressure in liquids_. __LEARN THEM__:

> 1) __PRESSURE IS _TRANSMITTED THROUGHOUT THE LIQUID___, so that the force can easily be applied __WHEREVER YOU WANT IT__, using flexible pipes.
>
> 2) The force can be __MULTIPLIED__ according to the __AREAS__ of the pistons used.

Hydraulic Jack

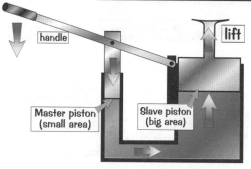

Car Brakes

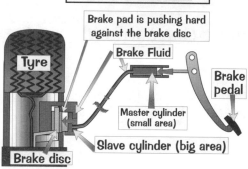

1) All hydraulic systems use a __SMALL__ master piston and a __BIG slave piston__.
2) The _master piston_ is used to apply a _force_, which puts the liquid _under pressure_.
3) This pressure is _transmitted_ throughout __all__ the liquid in the system, and somewhere _at the other end_ it pushes on the _slave piston_, which _exerts a force_ where it's needed.
4) The _slave piston_ always has a _much larger area_ than the _master piston_ so that it exerts a _much greater force_ from the pressure created by the force on the master piston. Clever stuff.
5) In this way, _hydraulic systems_ are _force multipliers_. i.e., they use a _small force_ to create a _very big force_ — a nice trick if you can do it.

The Typical Method for the Typical Exam Question:

1) Use the _master cylinder area_ and _force_ to calculate __THE PRESSURE IN THE SYSTEM__, P = F/A
2) Apply this pressure to the _area of the slave piston_ to calculate the __FORCE EXERTED__, F = P×A

__EXAMPLE:__ The car master piston has an area of 4cm². If a force of 400N is applied to it, calculate the pressure created in the brake pipes. If the slave piston has an area of 40cm², calculate the force exerted on the brake disc.

__ANSWER:__ At the _master piston_: Pressure created = F/A = 400N÷4cm² = 100N/cm² (not pascals!)
At the _slave piston_: Force produced = P×A = 100×40 = 4,000 (10 times original force)

Learn about hydraulics — and make light work of it...

You certainly need to know that formula for pressure, but that's pretty easy. The really tricky bit that you need to concentrate most on is how the formula is applied (twice) to explain how hydraulic systems turn a small force into a big one. _Keep working at it till you understand it._

Pressure in Gases

Volume Is Inversely Proportional to Pressure

This sounds a lot more confusing than it actually is. Here is the fancy definition:

When the **PRESSURE IS INCREASED** on a *fixed mass of gas* kept at *constant temperature*, the **VOLUME WILL DECREASE**. The changes in pressure and volume are in **INVERSE PROPORTION**.

If you ask me it's a pretty *obvious* way for a gas to behave. In simple language it's just this:

If you squash a gas into a smaller space, the pressure goes up in proportion to how much you squash it. e.g. if you squash it to half the amount of space, it'll end up at twice the pressure it was before (so long as you don't let it get hotter or colder, or let any escape). Simple, innit?

It can work the *other way* too. If you *increase the PRESSURE*, the *volume must DECREASE*. If you *increase the VOLUME*, the *pressure must DECREASE*. That's all pretty obvious though isn't it?

Gas Syringe Experiments Are Good for Showing This Law

1) A *gas syringe* makes a pretty good *airtight seal* and is great for demonstrating this law.

2) You put *weights on the top* to give a *definite* known force pushing down on the piston.

3) If you *double the weight*, you also double the *force*, which doubles the *pressure*.

4) You can then measure the *volume change* using the *scale* on the side of the syringe. Easy peasy.

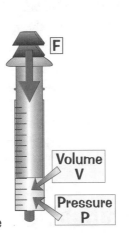

Using the Formula "$P_1V_1 = P_2V_2$"

Well what can I say, it's another formula. Not quite one you can put in a triangle, but still the same old idea: *stick in the numbers* they give you, and *work out the value* for the remaining letter. Please try and get it into your head that you don't need to *fully understand* the Physics, you just need a bit of "common sense" about *formulae*. Understanding always helps of course, but you can still get the right answer without it! Really, you've just got to identify the values for each letter — the rest is *very routine*.

EXAMPLE: A gas is compressed from a volume of 300cm³ at a pressure of 2.5 atmospheres down to a volume of 175cm³. Find the new pressure, in atmospheres.

ANSWER: "$P_1V_1 = P_2V_2$" gives: $2.5 \times 300 = P_2 \times 175$, so $P_2 = (2.5 \times 300) \div 175 = 4.3$ atm.

N.B. For *this formula*, always keep the units *the same* as they give them (in this case, pressure in *atmospheres*).

Less space, more collisions, more pressure — just like London...

This is another topic that can seem a lot more confusing than it really is. The basic principle of the law is simple enough, and so is the Gas Syringe demo. The formula might look bad but really there's nothing to it. In the end it's just stuff that needs *learning*, that's all. *Scribble*.

Sound Waves

1) Sound Travels as a Wave:

Sound can be _reflected_ off walls (echoes), and it can be _refracted_ as it passes into different media. These are standard properties of waves, so we deduce that _sound travels as a wave_. This "sound" reasoning can also be applied to deduce the wave nature of light.

2) Sound Waves Travel at Different Speeds in Different Media

1) _Sound Waves_ are caused by _vibrating_ objects.
2) Sound waves are _longitudinal_ waves that travel at _fixed speeds_ in particular _media_, as shown in the table.
3) As you can see, the _denser_ the medium, the _faster_ sound travels through it, generally speaking anyway.
4) Sound generally travels _faster in solids_ than in liquids, and faster in liquids than in gases.

Substance	Density	Speed of Sound
Iron	7.9 g/cm³	5000 m/s
Rubber	0.9 g/cm³	1600 m/s
Water	1.0 g/cm³	1400 m/s
Cork	0.3 g/cm³	500 m/s
Air	0.001 g/cm³	330 m/s

3) Sound Doesn't Travel Through a Vacuum

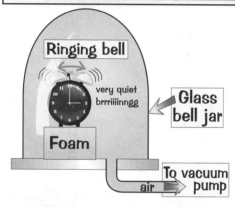

1) Sound waves can be _reflected_, _refracted_ and _diffracted_.
2) But one thing they _can't do_ is travel through a _vacuum_.
3) This is nicely demonstrated by the jolly old _bell jar experiment_.
4) As the air is _sucked out_ by the _vacuum pump_, the sound gets _quieter and quieter_.
5) The bell has to be _mounted_ on something like _foam_ to stop the sound from it travelling through the solid surface and making the bench vibrate, because you'd hear that instead.

4) Echoes and Reverberation Are Due to REFLECTED Sound

1) Sound will only be _reflected_ from _hard flat surfaces_. Things like _carpets_ and _curtains_ act as _absorbing surfaces_, which will _absorb_ sounds rather than reflect them.
2) This is very noticeable in the _reverberation_ of an _empty room_. A big empty room sounds _completely different_ once you've added carpet and curtains and a bit of furniture, because these things absorb the sound quickly and stop it _echoing_ (reverberating) around the room.

5) Amplitude Is a Measure of the Energy Carried by a Wave

1) The greater the _AMPLITUDE_, the _more ENERGY_ the wave carries.
2) With _SOUND_ this means it'll be _LOUDER_.
3) _Bigger amplitude_ means a _louder sound_.
4) With _LIGHT_, a bigger amplitude means it'll be _BRIGHTER_.

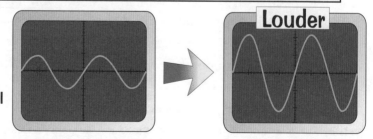

If sound travelled through vacuum — sunny days would be deafening...

Once again the page is broken up into five sections with numbered points for each. All those numbered points are important. They're all mentioned specifically in the syllabus so you should expect them to test exactly this stuff in the Exams. _Learn and enjoy._

Sound Waves

The Frequency of a Sound Wave Determines Its Pitch

1) _High frequency sound waves_ sound _HIGH PITCHED_ like a _squeaking mouse_.
2) _Low frequency_ sound waves sound _LOW PITCHED_ like a _mooing cow_.
3) _Frequency_ is the number of complete _vibrations_ each second. It's measured in _hertz_ (_Hz_).
4) Other common units are _kHz_ (1,000 Hz) and _MHz_ (1,000,000 Hz).
5) _High frequency_ (or high pitch) also means _shorter wavelength_.
6) The range of frequencies heard by humans is from about 20Hz to 20kHz.
7) These _CRO screens_ are _very important_, so make sure you know all about them:

The CRO screens tell us about the _pitch_ and _loudness_ of the sound:

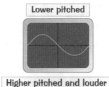

2) When the peaks are _further apart_ then the sound is at a _lower pitch_ (a lower frequency).

1) The _closer_ the peaks are, the _higher_ pitched the sound (and the _higher_ the frequency).

3) The CRO screen will show _large peaks_ for a _loud noise_ (sound waves with a _big amplitude_).

Microphones and Loudspeakers Convert Sound to and from Electrical Signals

An electrical _"signal"_ is simply a _varying electrical current_. The _variations_ in the current carry the _information_. The currents from a _microphone_ are _very small_ and are amplified into _much bigger signals_ by an amplifier. These _signals_ from the microphone can be _recorded_ and played back through _speakers_, in which the electric signal is used to move the _cone_ in and out, producing _sound_.

Echo Questions — Don't Forget the Factor of Two

1) The _big thing_ to remember with _echo questions_ is that because the sound has to travel _both ways_, then to get the _right answer_ you'll need to either _double something_ or _halve something_.
2) Make sure you remember: sound travels at about _330m/s in air_ and _1,400m/s in water_.
   Any echo question will likely be in air or water and if you have to work out the speed of the sound it's real useful to know what sort of number you should be getting.
   So for example, if you get 170m/s for the speed of sound in air then you should realise you've _forgotten the factor of two_ somewhere, and then you can _easily go back and sort it_.

EXAMPLE: Having successfully expelled the five most troublesome and nauseating kids from his school, the jubilant Headmaster popped open a bottle of Champagne and heard the echo 0.6s later from the other side of his modest office. Just how big was this modest office?

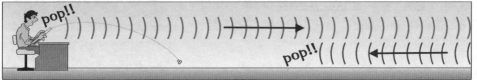

ANSWER: The formula is of course "Speed = Distance/Time" or "s=d/t". We want to find the distance, d. We already know the time, 0.6s, and the speed (of sound in air), hence d=s×t (from the triangle). This gives: d = 330×0.6 = _198m_. But Watch out! _Don't forget the factor of two for echo questions:_ The 0.6 secs is for _there and back_, so the office is only _half_ that distance — _99m long_.

Pitch — doesn't that have something to do with football...

Just three sections here, but its important stuff. And the simple truth is that you've just gotta know it if you want those Exam marks. You do realise I hope that _most Exam questions_, even in Physics, simply test whether or not you've _learned the basic facts_. Just _easy marks_ really.

68

Ultrasound

Sound

Ultrasound Is Sound with a Higher Frequency Than We Can Hear

Devices can be made that produce _electrical oscillations_ at virtually _any frequency_. These can easily be converted into _mechanical vibrations_ to produce _sound_ waves _beyond the range_ of _human hearing_ (i.e. frequencies above 20kHz). This is called _ULTRASOUND_, and it has loads of uses, like these:

Detecting with Ultrasound

1) The ultrasound waves are _transmitted_ through a _metal casting_ and whenever they reach the boundary between two _media_ (like metal and air), some of the wave is _reflected back_ and detected at the surface. The wave will reflect from the cracks in the casting because of the change in medium from metal to air.
2) The rest of the wave _continues_ through the casting and _more of the wave_ is reflected back (as echoes) at each _boundary_.
3) The exact _timing and distribution_ of these _echoes_ give detailed _information_ about the internal _structure_ of the casting.
4) The details are then _processed_ by _computer_ to produce a _visual display_ of the casting.

Two other uses for ultrasound:

1) Foetal Imaging

In pre-natal scanning the skin will normally reflect most of the ultrasound, so _saline gel_ is applied to the skin to improve the _transmission_ of the ultrasound.

The sound waves will pass through the skin and _reflect_ from the _surface of the foetus_.

These reflected waves are _detected_ at the _probe_ and converted into a _visual display_.

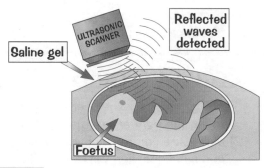

2) Range and Direction Finding — SONAR

Bats send out _high-pitched squeaks_ (ultrasound) and pick up the _reflections_ with their _big ears_. Their brains are able to _process_ the reflected signal and turn it into a _picture_ of what's around.
So the bats basically _"see"_ with _sound waves_, well enough in fact to catch _moths_ in _mid-flight_ in complete _darkness_ — it's a nice trick if you can do it.

The same technique is used for _SONAR_, which uses _sound waves underwater_ to detect features on the sea-bed. The _pattern_ of the reflections indicates the _depth_ and basic features.

Ultrasound — weren't they a pop group...

Geesh — you wouldn't think there was much more to say on sound by now. But ultrasound often appears in those lovely Exams, so I'd suggest you learn it. Start with the headings, then learn the points below each, _cover the page_, and _scribble a mini-essay_ for each, with diagrams.

SEG SYLLABUS

MODULE EIGHT — USING POWER

Revision Summary for Module Eight

More jolly questions that I know you're going to really enjoy. There are lots of bits and bobs on electricity, forces and waves that you definitely need to know. Some bits are certainly quite tricky to understand, but there's also loads of straightforward stuff that just needs to be learnt, ready for instant regurgitation in the Exam. You have to practise these questions over and over and over again, until you can answer them all really easily — phew, such jolly fun.

1) Sketch magnetic fields for: a) a bar magnet, b) a solenoid, c) two magnets attracting, d) two magnets repelling, e) the Earth's magnetic field, f) a current-carrying wire.
2) What is an electromagnet made from? Explain how to work out the polarity of the ends.
3) What is meant by magnetically "soft"?
4) Sketch and give details of: a) relay b) electric bell.
5) Sketch two demos of the motor effect. Sketch a simple motor and list four ways to speed it up.
6) Describe the three details of Fleming's left hand rule. What is it used for?
7) Sketch the two types of transformer, and highlight the main details. Explain how they work.
8) Write down the transformer equation. Do your own worked example — it's ace practice.
9) Sketch a typical power station and the National Grid, and explain why it's at 400kV.
10) What is static electricity? What is nearly always the cause of it building up?
11) Which particles move when static builds up, and which ones don't?
12) Give *one* example of static being: a) helpful b) a little joker c) terrorist.
13) What's the unit used for electric charge. What's the formula used to calculate it?
14) Sketch a view of a circuit to explain the formula "E=QV". Which dull definitions go with it?
15) Define electrical power, and state its formula.
16) What's the connection between "work done" and "energy transferred"?
17) What's the formula for work done?
18) What's the formula for power? What are the units of power?
19) Write down the formulae for KE and PE.
20) What's the difference between speed and velocity? Give an example of each.
21) What's acceleration? What are its units? Write down its formula.
22) Write down the First Law of Motion. Illustrate it with a diagram.
23) Write down the Second Law of Motion. Illustrate it with a diagram. What's the formula for it?
24) Explain what "resultant force" is. Illustrate it with a diagram. When do you most need it?
25) Write down the Third Law of Motion. Illustrate it with four diagrams.
26) Explain what reaction force is and where it pops up.
27) Explain what friction is, and name two different types. Give an example for each.
28) What are the two different parts of the overall stopping distance of a car?
29) List the three or four factors that affect each part of the stopping distance.
30) Which formula explains why the stopping distance increases so much? Explain why it does.
31) What's the definition of pressure? What combination of force and area gives high pressure?
32) What happens to pressure as you go deeper? Which direction does the pressure act in?
33) What's the formula for pressure? What units is pressure given in? What's the definition?
34) Write down the two features of pressure in liquids that allow hydraulic systems to work.
35) Sketch a jack and a car braking system and explain how they work as force multipliers.
36) What is the pressure law? Sketch an experiment that demonstrates it. What's the formula?
37) Write down some typical speeds for sound in different materials.
38) Describe the bell jar experiment. What does it demonstrate?
39) What's an echo? What is reverberation? What affects reverberation in a room?
40) What's the connection between amplitude and the energy carried by a wave?
41) What effect does greater amplitude have on a) sound waves b) light waves?
42) What's the relationship between frequency and pitch for a sound wave?
43) Sketch CRO screens showing high and low pitch, and quiet and loud sounds.
44) What is ultrasound? Give details of two applications of ultrasound.

The Origin of the Universe

The *Big Bang theory* is our most <u>convincing</u> theory of the origin of the Universe — though it's not the only one.

Red-Shift Needs Explaining

There are <u>TWO important bits of evidence</u> you need to know about:

1) Light from Other Galaxies Is Red-Shifted

1) When we look at <u>light</u> from distant <u>galaxies</u> we find that <u>all the frequencies</u> are <u>shifted</u> towards the <u>red end</u> of the spectrum.
2) In other words the <u>frequencies</u> are all <u>slightly lower</u> than they should be. This is because the galaxies are all <u>moving away from us</u>. It's the same effect as a car <u>horn</u> sounding lower-pitched when the car is travelling <u>away</u> from you. The sound <u>drops in frequency</u>.
3) This is called the <u>Doppler effect</u>.
4) <u>Measurements</u> of the red-shift suggest that <u>all</u> the distant galaxies are <u>moving away from us</u> very quickly — and it's the <u>same</u> whatever direction you look in.

2) The Further Away a Galaxy Is , the Greater the Red-Shift

1) <u>More distant galaxies</u> have <u>greater</u> red-shifts than nearer ones.
2) This means that more distant galaxies are <u>moving away faster</u> than nearer ones.
3) The <u>inescapable conclusion</u> appears to be that the whole Universe is <u>expanding</u>.

The Big Bang Theory — How It All Started

1) Since all the galaxies appear to be <u>moving apart</u> very rapidly, the obvious <u>conclusion</u> is that there was an <u>initial explosion</u>: the <u>Big Bang</u>.
2) All the matter in the Universe must have been <u>compressed</u> into a <u>very small space</u>, which then rapidly expanded. The <u>expansion</u> is still going on today.
3) The Big Bang is believed to have happened around <u>15 billion years ago</u>.
4) The age of the Universe can be <u>estimated</u> from the current rate of <u>expansion</u>.
5) These estimates are <u>not very accurate</u> because it's hard to tell how much the expansion has <u>slowed down</u> since the Big Bang.
6) The rate at which the expansion is <u>slowing down</u> is an <u>important factor</u> in deciding the <u>future</u> of the Universe.
7) <u>Without gravity</u> the Universe would expand at the <u>same rate forever</u>.
8) However, the <u>attraction</u> between all the mass in the Universe tends to <u>slow</u> the expansion down.

Red shift — it's all in black and white before you...

The thing to learn here is the importance of <u>red shift</u>. It's what tells us that the Universe must have had a beginning. So <u>learn</u> all those little points, then <u>cover them up</u> and <u>jot them down</u>, then on your lunch-break you can ponder the mysteries of the universe over those sarnies.

The Life Cycle of Stars

Stars go through _many traumatic stages_ in their lives — just like teenagers.

Clouds of Dust and Gas

1) Stars _initially form_ from clouds of _DUST AND GAS_.

Protostar

2) The _force of gravity_ makes the dust particles come _spiralling in together_. As they do, _gravitational energy_ is converted into _heat energy_ and the _temperature rises_.

Main Sequence Star

3) When the _temperature_ gets _high enough_, _hydrogen nuclei_ undergo _nuclear fusion_ to form _helium nuclei_ and give out massive amounts of _heat and light_. A star is born. It immediately enters a long _stable period_ in which the _heat created_ by the nuclear fusion provides an _outward pressure_ to _BALANCE_ the _force of gravity_ pulling everything _inwards_. The Sun's presently in the middle of its stable period, and luckily for us it's still got about _5 billion years_ to go. (Or to put it another way, the _Earth's_ already had _HALF its innings_ before the Sun _engulfs_ it!)

Red Giant

4) Eventually the _hydrogen_ begins to _run out_ and the star then _swells_ into a _RED GIANT_. It becomes _red_ because the surface _cools_. At this stage the Sun's surface will reach out to _past the Earth's present orbit_, and the Earth will be _swallowed up_. Still, at least it won't happen for a _few more billion years_...

5) A _SMALL STAR_ like our Sun will then begin to _cool_ and _contract_ into a _WHITE DWARF_. The _matter_ from which _white dwarfs_ are made is _MILLIONS OF TIMES DENSER_ than any matter on Earth because the _gravity is so strong_ it even crushes the _atoms_. A white dwarf is about the _size of the Earth_, yet it contains virtually all the _mass_ of the _original star_.

Big stars   Small stars

White Dwarf

Supernova

6) _BIG STARS_ on the other hand will eventually _explode_ in a _SUPERNOVA_, providing gas and dust to start the whole process again...

Twinkle twinkle little star, how I wond.. — JUST LEARN IT PAL...

Erm. Just how do they know all that? As if it's not outrageous enough that they reckon to know the whole history of the Earth for the last five billion years, they also reckon to know the whole life cycle of stars, when they're all billions and billions of km away. It's just an outrage.

The Evolution of the Atmosphere

The present composition of the atmosphere is: _78% Nitrogen_, _21% oxygen_, _0.03% CO$_2$_ (= 99.03%). The remaining 1% is made up of noble gases (mainly argon). In addition there can be a lot of water vapour. But the atmosphere wasn't _always_ like this. Here's how the first 4.5 billion years have gone:

Phase 1 — Volcanoes gave out Steam, CO$_2$, NH$_3$ and CH$_4$

1) The Earth's surface was originally _molten_ for many millions of years. Any atmosphere _boiled away_.
2) Eventually it cooled and a thin crust formed but _volcanoes_ kept erupting.
3) They belched out mostly _carbon dioxide_.
4) But also some _steam_, _ammonia_ and _methane_.
5) The early atmosphere was _mostly_ CO$_2$.
6) There was virtually _no_ oxygen.
7) The water vapour _condensed_ to form the _oceans_.
8) _Holiday report:_ Not a nice place to be. Take strong walking boots and a good coat.

Phase 2 — Green Plants Evolved and produced Oxygen

1) Green _plants_ evolved over most of the Earth.
2) They were quite happy in the _CO$_2$ atmosphere_.
3) A lot of the early CO$_2$ _dissolved_ into the oceans.
4) But the green plants steadily _removed_ CO$_2$ and _produced_ O$_2$.
5) Much of the CO$_2$ from the air thus became locked up in _fossil fuels_ and _sedimentary rocks_.
6) _Methane_ and _ammonia_ reacted with the _oxygen_, releasing _nitrogen_ gas.
7) Ammonia was also converted into _nitrates_ by nitrifying bacteria. Some nitrates were then converted into _proteins_ by plants.
8) _Nitrogen_ gas was also released by _living organisms_ like denitrifying bacteria.
9) _Holiday Report:_ A bit slimy underfoot. Take wellies and a lot of suncream.

Phase 3 — Ozone Layer allows Evolution of Complex Animals

1) The build-up of _oxygen_ in the atmosphere _killed off_ early organisms that couldn't tolerate it.
2) It also enabled the _evolution_ of more _complex_ organisms that made use of the oxygen.
3) The oxygen also created the _ozone layer_ (O$_3$) which _blocked_ harmful rays from the Sun and _enabled_ even more _complex_ organisms to evolve.
4) There is virtually _no CO$_2$_ left now.
5) _Holiday report:_ A nice place to be. Get there before the crowds ruin it.

Coo... 4½ billion years — just takes your breath away...

I think it's pretty amazing how much the atmosphere has changed. It makes our present day obsession about the CO$_2$ going up from 0.03% to 0.04% seem a bit ridiculous, doesn't it! Anyway, never mind that, just _learn the three phases with all their details_. You don't have to draw the diagrams — although thinking about it, it's a pretty good way to remember it all, don't you think. Yip.

Higher Higher Higher

The Nitrogen and Carbon Cycles

The Nitrogen Cycle

1) There's *another version* of this in Module 6 (P. 25), since most of these processes are *biological*. The two diagrams (this one and the one in Module 6) may *look* completely different but they're pretty much *the same* underneath it all. It's just that things are *positioned* differently. This one is in typical Exam style — i.e. hard to understand.

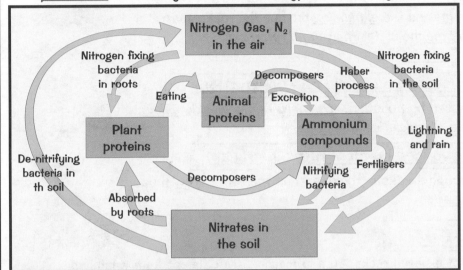

2) However, the *processes* are all the *same*, and that's the important bit.

3) In the Exam they can give you *any version* of the carbon or nitrogen cycle that they feel like and you have to able to relate it to the diagrams you already know.

4) Once you *properly understand* one version, you can do *any*. In principle.

The Carbon Cycle

1) There's *another version* of the carbon cycle given in Module 6 (P. 24) which is much prettier.

2) There are *many* different ways of representing the carbon cycle, but in the end *they all show the same things happening*. If you *properly understand* one diagram you should be able to deal with any other, even if it looks totally different. Apart from the pretty colours this is a *standard syllabus version*. That means it's like the one you'll likely get in your Exam.

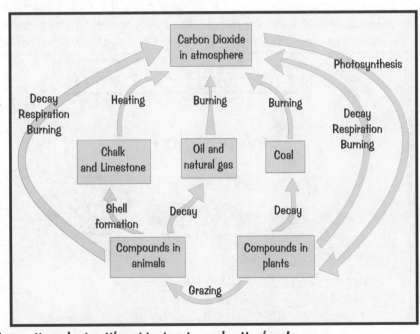

3) This diagram just shows all the information, but *without* trying to make it *clear*! Look at how this relates to the one in Module 6, which does try to make it clear.

4) This one also contains *chalk* and *limestone* which were left out of the biology one.

5) You should learn about all these processes elsewhere. This diagram is just a *summary* of them.

6) The Carbon cycle is how the level of carbon dioxide in the atmosphere is maintained.

7) In the Exam they could give you this diagram with *labels missing* and you'd have to *explain* or *describe* the missing process, so it's *pretty important* that you understand the *whole* thing and know about each process.

Learn and Enjoy...

The nitrogen and carbon cycles — tip top for entertainment value.

Weathering and the Water Cycle

(Sounds like an episode from "Last of The Summer Wine" — you can just picture the whole 30 minutes of it...)

Weathering is the process of breaking rocks up

There are _three_ distinct ways that rocks are _broken up_ into small _fragments_:

A) Physical weathering is caused by ice in cracks

1) _Rain water_ seeps into _cracks_ in rocks and if the temperature drops _below freezing_, the water turns to _ice_ and the _expansion_ pushes the rocks apart.
2) This keeps happening _each time_ the water _thaws and refreezes_.
3) Eventually bits of rock will _break off_.

B) Chemical Weathering is caused by acidic rain on limestone

This isn't just "acid rain" caused by pollution. _Ordinary rain_ is _weakly acidic_ anyway, so it very gradually _dissolves_ all _limestone_.

C) Biological weathering is caused by plant roots in cracks

Plants push their _roots_ through cracks in rocks and as the roots _grow_ they gradually _push the rocks apart_.

Erosion and Transport

1) _Erosion_ is the _wearing away_ of exposed rocks, by any means. It's different from weathering.
2) _Transport_ is the process of _carrying away_ the rock fragments, either _falling away_ due to gravity, or being carried away _by rivers_. The rocks travelling down rivers get _worn down_ as they go and they also wear away the _river bed_ causing _river valleys_. The Grand Canyon is a grand example.

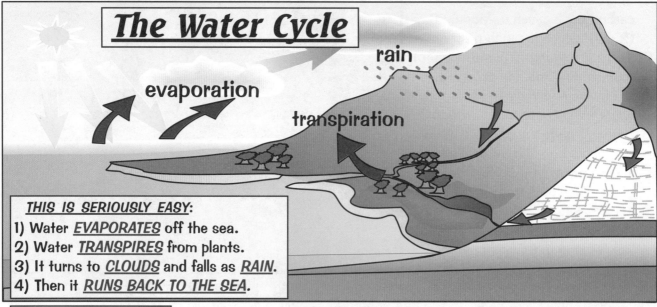

The Water Cycle

rain

evaporation

transpiration

THIS IS SERIOUSLY EASY:
1) Water _EVAPORATES_ off the sea.
2) Water _TRANSPIRES_ from plants.
3) It turns to _CLOUDS_ and falls as _RAIN_.
4) Then it _RUNS BACK TO THE SEA_.

FOUR EXTRA DETAILS: (which are only very slightly harder to remember than the diagram)

1) The _SUN_ causes the _evaporation_ of water from the sea.
2) _Clouds form_ because: when _air rises_, it _cools_, and the _water condenses_ out.
3) When the condensed droplets get _too big_ they _fall as rain_.
4) Some water is taken up by _roots_ and _evaporates from trees_ without ever reaching the _sea_.

Page after page of sheer toil — it can wear you down...

Ooh, this is all really easy stuff isn't it. The only tricky bit is remembering the fancy words, like "erosion" and "chemical weathering", and exactly what they are. You know, "erosion" isn't quite the same as "weathering", for example.   It's the same old method though: _Learn it, then cover the page, etc._

The Rock Cycle

Rocks shouldn't be confusing. There are _three_ different types: _sedimentary_, _metamorphic_ and _igneous_. Over _millions_ of years they _change_ from one into another. This is called the _Rock Cycle_. Astonishingly.

The Rock Cycle

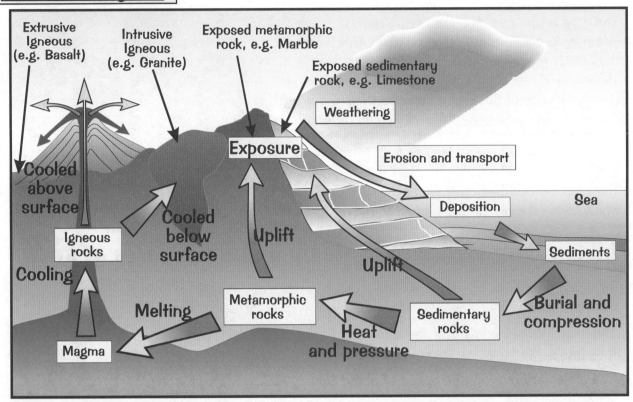

The Rocks Change from One to Another in a Slow Cycle

1) Particles get washed to the _sea_ and settle as _sediment_.

2) Over _millions_ of years these sediments get _crushed_ into **SEDIMENTARY** _rocks_ (hence the name).

3) At first they get _buried_, but they can either _rise_ to the surface again to be discovered, or they can _descend_ into the _heat_ and _pressure_ below.

4) If they _do_, the heat and pressure _completely alter_ the structure of the rock and they then become **METAMORPHIC ROCKS** (as in "metamorphosis" or "change". Another good name!).

5) These _metamorphic rocks_ can either rise to the _surface_ to be discovered by an enthusiastic geologist or else descend _still further_ into the fiery abyss of the Earth's raging inferno where they will _melt_ and become _magma_.

6) When _magma_ reaches the surface it _cools_ and _sets_ and is then called **IGNEOUS ROCK**.
   ("igneous" as in "ignite" or "fire" — another cool name. Gee, if only biology names were this sensible.)

7) There are actually _two types_ of igneous rock:
   1) **EXTRUSIVE** when it comes _straight out_ of the surface from a _volcano_ ("Ex-" as in "Exit").
   2) **INTRUSIVE** when it just sets as a big lump _below_ the surface ("In-" as in "inside").
      (I have to say — whoever invented these names deserves a medal)

8) When any of these rocks reach the _surface_, then _weathering_ begins and they gradually get _worn down_ and carried off to the _sea_ and the whole cycle _starts over again_... Simple, innit?

Rocks are a mystery — no, no, it's sedimentary my Dear Watson...

Don't you think the Rock Cycle is pretty ace? Can you think of anything you'd rather do than go on a family holiday to Cornwall, gazing at the cliffs and marvelling at the different types of rocks and stuff? Exactly. (And even if you can, it's still a good plan to _learn about rocks_.)

Plate Tectonics

Crust, Mantle, Outer and Inner Core

1) The _crust_ is very _thin_ (well, about 20km or so!).
2) The _mantle_ is _liquid_ but very _viscous_.
3) The _core_ is just over _half_ the Earth's radius.
4) The _core_ is made from _iron_ and _nickel_. This is where the Earth's _magnetic field_ originates.
5) The iron and nickel _sank_ to the "bottom" long ago (i.e. the centre of the Earth) because they're _denser_.
6) The core has a _solid inner_ bit and a _liquid outer_ bit.

Higher

7) Natural _radioactive decay_ creates a lot of the _heat_ inside the Earth.
8) This heat causes the _convection currents_ which cause the plates of the crust to move.

Higher

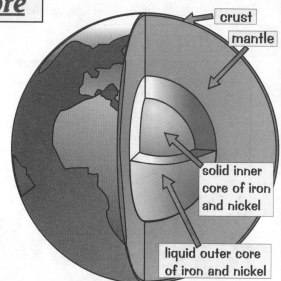

crust
mantle
solid inner core of iron and nickel
liquid outer core of iron and nickel

The Earth's Surface is made up of Large Plates of Rock

1) These _plates_ are like _big rafts_ that float across the liquid mantle.

2) The map shows the _edges_ of these plates. As they _move_, the _continents_ move too.

3) The plates are moving at a speed of about 1cm or 2cm _per year_.

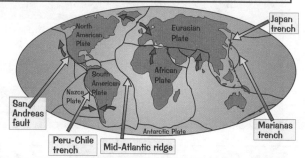

North American Plate
Eurasian Plate
Japan trench
South American Plate
African Plate
Nazca Plate
San Andreas fault
Peru-Chile trench
Mid-Atlantic ridge
Antarctic Plate
Marianas trench

At the _boundaries_ between tectonic plates there's usually trouble like _volcanoes_ or _earthquakes_. There are _three_ different ways that plates interact: _Colliding_, _separating_ or _sliding_ past each other.

Plates Sliding Past Each Other: San Francisco

1) Sometimes the plates are just _sliding_ past each other.
2) The best known example of this is the _San Andreas Fault_ in California.
3) A narrow strip of the coastline is sliding north at about _7cm a year_.
4) Big plates of rock _don't glide smoothly_ past each other.
5) They _catch_ on each other and as the _forces build up_ they suddenly _lurch_.
6) This _sudden lurching_ only lasts _a few seconds_ — but it'll bring buildings down.
7) The city of _San Francisco_ sits _astride_ this fault line.
8) The city was _destroyed_ by an earthquake in _1906_ and hit by another quite serious one in _1991_. They could have another one any time.
9) In _earthquake zones_ they try to build _earthquake-proof_ buildings which are designed to withstand a bit of shaking.
10) Earthquakes usually cause _much greater devastation_ in _poorer countries_ where they may have _overcrowded cities_, _poorly constructed buildings_, and _inadequate rescue services_.

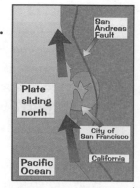

San Andreas Fault
Plate sliding north
City of San Francisco
California
Pacific Ocean

Try telling that lot to the Spanish Inquisition...

More _nice easy stuff_. That means it's nice easy marks in the Exam too. They do put easy stuff in, just so that everyone gets at least some marks. Just make sure you learn _ALL_ the details. There's _nothing dafter_ than missing easy marks. _Cover the page and check you know it ALL._

Plate Tectonics

Oceanic and Continental Plates Colliding: The Andes

1) The _oceanic_ plate is always forced _underneath_ the continental plate.
2) This is called a _subduction zone_.
3) As the oceanic crust is pushed down it _melts_ and _pressure_ builds up due to all the melting rock.
4) This _molten rock_ finds its way to the surface and _volcanoes_ form.
5) There are also _earthquakes_ as the two plates slowly _grind_ past each other.
6) A deep _trench_ forms on the ocean floor where the _oceanic plate_ is being _forced_ down.
7) The _continental_ crust _crumples_ and _folds_ forming _mountains_ at the coast.
8) The classic example of all this is the west coast of _South America_ where the _Andes mountains_ are. That region has _all_ the features:

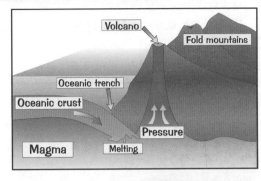

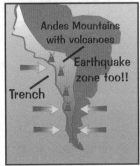

> _Volcanoes_, _earthquakes_, an _oceanic trench_ and _mountains_.

Sea Floor Spreading: The Mid-Atlantic Ridge

1) When tectonic plates move apart, _magma_ rises up to fill the gap and produces _new crust_ made of _basalt_ (of course). Sometimes it comes out with great _force_ producing _undersea volcanoes_.
2) The _Mid-Atlantic ridge_ runs the whole length of the Atlantic and actually cuts through the middle of _Iceland_, which is why they have _hot underground water_.
3) Earthquakes and volcanoes under the sea can cause massive _tidal waves_ (_tsunami_). These waves can cause great destruction.
4) The magma rises up through the gap and forms _ridges_ and _underwater mountains_.
5) These form a _symmetrical pattern_ either side of the ridge, providing strong _evidence_ for the theory of _continental drift_.

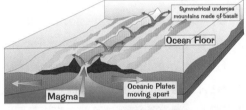

The Rock Record Tells Us the Earth's Dim and Distant Past

1) _Sedimentary_ rocks usually form _layers_ — with the _older_ rocks at the _bottom_ and the _younger_ ones on _top_. The same _sequences_ commonly occur over _large areas_, but they're often _distorted_ — and sometimes even _upside down_. Pretty good evidence for _geological change_, I'd say.
2) _Sedimentary rocks_ can be _dated_ by looking at the types of _fossils_ they contain, while _radioactive dating_ can be used for many _igneous rocks_. The positions of rocks can also tell you a lot, e.g. if an igneous rock _cuts across_ another rock, then it's pretty obvious the other rock must be _older_.
3) All this _evidence_ for past geological changes and their sequence is called the ROCK RECORD.

Another page to learn — don't make a mountain out of it...

Make sure you learn all these diagrams — they summarise all the information in the text.
They may well ask you for examples in the Exam, so make sure you know the two different kinds of situation that the Andes and San Francisco actually represent. _Cover and scribble..._

Sedimentary Rocks

Three steps in the Formation of Sedimentary Rocks

1) _Sedimentary rocks_ are formed from _layers of sediment_ laid down in _lakes_ or _seas_.

2) Over _millions of years_ the layers get buried under more layers and the _weight_ pressing down _squeezes_ out the water.

3) As the water disappears, _salts_ crystallize out and _cement_ the particles together.

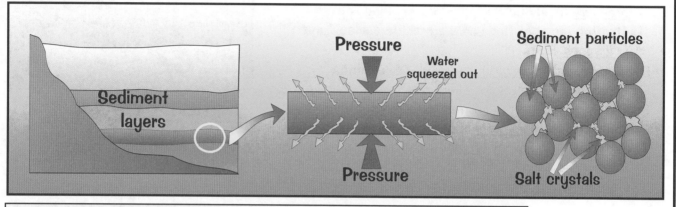

Fossils are only found in Sedimentary Rocks

1) Only _sedimentary_ rocks contain _fossils_. The other two types of rock, metamorphic and igneous, have been through too much _heat and trauma_ to have fossils left in them.

2) Sedimentary rocks have only been _gently crushed_ for a few million years. No big deal, so the fossils _survive_. All sedimentary rocks are likely to contain fossils.

3) Fossils are a very useful way of _identifying rocks_ as being of the _same age_.

4) This is because fossilised remains that are found _change_ (due to evolution) as the _ages pass_.

5) This means that if two rocks have the _same fossils_ they are probably from the _same age_.

6) However, if the fossils in two rocks are _different_, it proves _nothing_ don't forget!

The Three Main Sedimentary Rocks:

Sedimentary rocks tend to look similar to the _original sediments_ from which they formed. After all, _very little_ has happened other than them _squashing_ together.

1) Sandstone

This is formed from _sand_ of course. And it looks like it too. Sandstone just looks like _sand particles_ all stuck very firmly together. There's _red_ sandstone and _yellow_ sandstone which are commonly used for _buildings_. The now famous Barrow Town Hall is built in red sandstone.

2) Limestone

This formed from _seashells_. It's mostly _calcium carbonate_ and _grey/white_ in colour. The original _shells_ are mostly _crushed_ but there are still quite a few _fossilised shells_ to be found in _limestone_.

3) Mudstone or shale

This was formed from _mud_ which basically means _finer_ particles than _sand_. It's often _dark grey_ and tends to _split_ into the _original layers_ very easily.

Revision pressure — don't get crushed by it...

Quite a lot of facts here on sedimentary rocks. You've gotta _learn_ how they form, that they contain fossils, and also the names etc. of the four examples. Most important you need to be able to _describe_ in words _what they all look like_. Even if you don't really know, just learn the descriptions!

Metamorphic Rocks

Heat and Pressure over Thousands of Years

Metamorphic rocks are formed by the action of _heat_ and _pressure_ on existing (_sedimentary_) rocks over _long_ periods of time.

1) _Earth movements_ can push all types of rock _deep_ underground.

2) Here they are compressed and heated, and the _mineral structure_ and _texture_ may change.

3) So long as they don't actually _melt_ they are classed as _metamorphic_ rocks.

4) _If they melt_ and turn to _magma_, they're _gone_. The magma may resurface as igneous rocks.

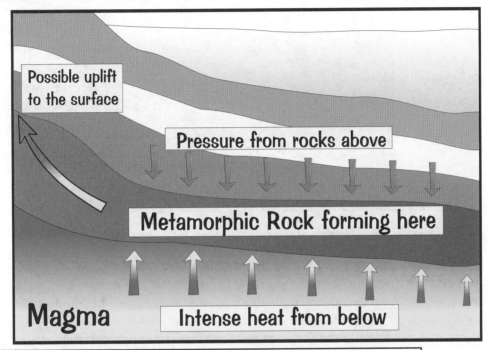

Slate and Marble are Metamorphic Rocks

1) Slate is formed from mudstone or clay

1) As the mudstone gets _heated_ and _compressed_ its tiny _plate-like_ particles align in the _same direction_.

2) This allows the resulting _slate_ to be _split_ along that direction into _thin sheets_ which make _ideal_ roofing material.

3) As it cools, it forms _miniscule_ crystals.

4) The increasingly famous Barrow Town Hall has a slate roof.

2) Marble is formed from Limestone

1) Very high temperature will break down the _shells_ in limestone and they reform as _small crystals_.

2) This gives marble a _more even texture_ and makes it much _harder_.

3) It can be _polished up_ and often has attractive patterning.

4) This makes it a great _decorative stone_. My Uncle Cyril has a fabulous Marble Headstone.

Chemistry's great — don't slate it...

There's quite a lot of names accumulating now. Somehow, you've got to make sense of them in your head. It really does help _if you know what these rocks actually look like_ in real life.
It's best if you can think of specific objects made of them. Otherwise, it'll all get pretty tricky.

Igneous Rocks

Igneous Rocks are formed from Fresh Magma

1) *Igneous rocks* form when *molten* magma pushes up into the *crust* or right *through it*.

2) Igneous rocks contain various different *minerals* in *randomly-arranged* interlocking *crystals*.

3) There are *two types* of igneous rocks: *EXTRUSIVE* and *INTRUSIVE*:

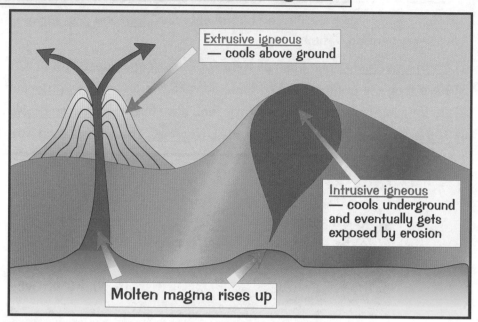

Extrusive igneous — cools above ground

Intrusive igneous — cools underground and eventually gets exposed by erosion

Molten magma rises up

INTRUSIVE igneous rocks cool SLOWLY with BIG crystals
GRANITE is an intrusive igneous rock with big crystals

1) *Granite* is formed *underground* where the magma cools down *slowly*.
2) This means it has *big* randomly-arranged *crystals* because it cools down *slowly*.
3) Granite is a very *hard* and *decorative* stone ideal for steps and buildings.
4) Barrow Town Hall?   Don't know.

EXTRUSIVE igneous rocks cool QUICKLY with SMALL crystals
BASALT is an extrusive igneous rock with small crystals

1) *Basalt* is formed *on top* of the Earth's crust after *bursting out* of a *volcano*.
2) This means it has *relatively small* crystals — because it *cooled quickly*.

Identifying Rocks in Exam Questions

A typical question will simply *describe* a rock and ask you to *identify it*. Make sure you learn the information on rocks well enough to work *backwards*, as it were, so that you can *identify* the type of rock from a description. *Practise* by doing these:

Rock A:	Small crystals in layers.
Rock B:	Contains fossils.
Rock C:	Randomly arranged crystals of various types.
Rock D:	Hard, smooth and with wavy layers of crystals.
Rock E:	Large crystals. Very hard wearing.
Rock F:	Sandy texture. Fairly soft.

Answers

A: metamorphic
B: sedimentary
C: igneous
D: metamorphic
E: igneous (granite)
F: Sedimentary (sandstone)

Igneous rocks are real cool — or they're magma...

It's very important that you know what granite looks like. You really should insist that "Teach" organises a field trip to see the famous pink granite coast of Brittany. About two weeks should be enough time to fully appreciate it. In May. Failing that, sit and *learn this page* in cold grey Britain for ten minutes.

Metal Ores from the Ground

Rocks, Minerals and Ores

1) A _rock_ is a mixture of _minerals_.
2) A _mineral_ is any _solid element or compound_ found naturally in the _Earth's crust_.
   Examples: Diamond (carbon), quartz (silicon dioxide), bauxite (Al_2O_3).
3) A _metal ore_ is defined as a _mineral_ or minerals which contain _enough metal_ in them to make it _worthwhile_ extracting the metal from it.

Metals are _Extracted_ using _Carbon_ or _Electrolysis_

1) _Extracting a metal_ from its ore involves a _chemical reaction_ to separate the metal out.
2) In many cases the metal is found as an _oxide_. There are three ores you need to know:

> a) _Iron ore_ is called _Haematite_, which is iron(III) oxide, formula Fe_2O_3.
> b) _Aluminium ore_ is called _Bauxite_, which is aluminium oxide, formula Al_2O_3.
> c) _Copper ore_ is called _Malachite_, which is copper(II) carbonate, formula $CuCO_3$.

3) The _TWO_ common ways of _extracting a metal_ from its ore are:
   a) Chemical _reduction_ using _carbon_ (this works for iron) or _carbon monoxide_
   b) _Electrolysis_ (breaking the ore down by passing an electric current through it).
4) _Gold_ is one of the few metals found as a _metal_ rather than in a chemical compound (an _ore_).

More Reactive Metals are Harder to Get

1) The _more reactive_ metals took _longer_ to be discovered (e.g. aluminium, sodium).
2) The _more reactive_ metals are also _harder to extract_ from their mineral ores.

The Position of Carbon in the Reactivity Series decides it...

1) Metals _higher than carbon_ in the reactivity series have to be extracted using _electrolysis_.
2) Metals _below carbon_ in the reactivity series can be extracted by _reduction_ using _carbon_.
3) This is obviously because carbon _can only take the oxygen_ away from metals which are _less reactive_ than carbon _itself_ is.

Extracted using _Electrolysis_

Extracted by _reduction_ using _carbon_

The Reactivity Series	
Potassium	K
Sodium	Na
Calcium	Ca
Magnesium	Mg
Aluminium	Al
CARBON	C
Zinc	Zn
Iron	Fe
Tin	Sn
Lead	Pb

Demand for Raw Materials

As we use more and more of the _raw materials_ needed to make metals (ores), the increased demand can cause some problems:

1) There's only a _limited_ amount in the Earth. As we use up known deposits, we have to find more, which are often more difficult and _expensive_ to mine.
2) New deposits may be a nice area of countryside. Large mines can make a beautiful spot really _ugly_.
3) Any metal we throw away has to be _disposed_ of. Land fill sites are also ugly, and metals don't rot like wood or paper.

Miners — they always have to get their ore in...

This page has four sections with three or four important points in each.
They're all important enough to need learning.
You need to practise _repeating_ the details _from memory_. That's the _only effective method_.

Iron — The Blast Furnace

Iron is a *very common element* in the Earth's crust, but good iron ores are only found in *a few select places* around the world, such as Australia, Canada and *Millom*.

Iron is extracted from *haematite*, Fe_2O_3, by *reduction* (i.e. removal of oxygen) in a *blast furnace*. You really do need to know all these details about what goes on in a blast furnace, *including the equations*.

The Raw Materials are Iron Ore, Coke and Limestone

1) The iron ore contains the *iron* (which is pretty important).
2) The *coke* is almost pure *carbon*. This is for *reducing* the *iron oxide* to *iron metal*.
3) The *limestone* takes away impurities in the form of *slag*.

Reducing the Iron Ore to Iron:

1) *Hot air* is blasted into the furnace making the coke *burn much faster* than usual and the *temperature rises* to about 1500°C.

2) The *coke burns* and produces *carbon dioxide*:

$$C + O_2 \rightarrow CO_2$$

3) The CO_2 then reacts with *unburnt coke* to form *CO*:

$$CO_2 + C \rightarrow 2CO$$

4) The *carbon monoxide* then *reduces* the *iron ore* to *iron*:

$$3CO + Fe_2O_3 \rightarrow 3CO_2 + 2Fe$$

5) The *iron* is of course *molten* at this temperature and it's also *dense* so it runs straight to the *bottom* of the furnace where it's *tapped off*.

Iron ore, coke and limestone

1500°C

Hot air

Removing the Impurities:

1) The *main impurity* is *sand* (silicon dioxide). This is still *solid* even at 1500°C and would tend to stay mixed in with the iron. The limestone removes it.

2) The limestone is *decomposed* by the *heat* into *calcium oxide* and CO_2.

$$CaCO_3 \rightarrow CaO + CO_2$$

3) The *calcium oxide* then reacts with the *sand* to form *calcium silicate* or *slag* which is molten and can be tapped off:

$$CaO + SiO_2 \rightarrow CaSiO_3 \text{ (molten slag)}$$

Molten iron   Molten slag

4) The cooled slag is *solid*, and is used for:
   1) *Road building*   2) *Fertiliser*

Iron is made into Steel which is cheap and strong

Iron and steel are used for:
1) *Construction* such as bridges and buildings.
2) *Cars* and *lorries* and *trains* and *boats* and NOT PLANES and *pushbikes* and *tanks* and *pianos*...
3) *Stainless steel* doesn't rust and is used for pans and for fixtures on boats.

Learn the facts about Iron Extraction — it's a blast...

Three main sections and several numbered points for each. Every bit of it is important and could be tested in the Exam, including the equations. Use the *mini-essay* method for each section. Alternatively, cover it up one section at a time, and try *repeating the facts* back to yourself. *And keep trying.*

Extracting Aluminium

A Molten State is needed for Electrolysis

1) _Aluminium_ is more _reactive_ than _carbon_ so it has to be extracted from its ore by _electrolysis_.

2) The basic ore is _bauxite_, and after mining and purifying a white powder is left.

3) This is pure aluminium oxide, Al_2O_3, which has a _very high_ melting point of over 2000°C.

4) For _electrolysis_ to work a _molten state_ is required, and heating to 2000°C would be _expensive_.

Cryolite is used to lower the temperature (and costs)

1) Instead, the aluminium oxide is _dissolved_ in _molten cryolite_ (a less common ore of aluminium).

2) This brings the temperature _down_ to about 900°C, which makes it _much_ cheaper and easier.

3) The _electrodes_ are made of _graphite_ (carbon).

4) The graphite _anode_ (+ve) does need _replacing_ quite often. It keeps _reacting_ to form CO_2.

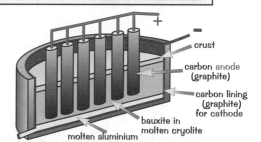

crust

carbon anode (graphite)

carbon lining (graphite) for cathode

bauxite in molten cryolite

molten aluminium

Electrolysis — turning IONS into the ATOMS you want

This is the _main object_ of the exercise:

1) Make the aluminium oxide _molten_ to _release_ the aluminium _ions_, Al^{3+} so they're _free_ to move.

2) Stick _electrodes_ in — so that the _positive Al^{3+} ions_ will head straight for the _negative electrode_.

3) At the negative electrode they just can't help picking up some of the _spare electrons_ and 'zup', they've turned into aluminium _atoms_ and they _sink to the bottom_.   Pretty clever, I think.

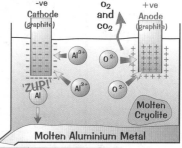

-ve Cathode (graphite)

O_2 and CO_2

+ve Anode (graphite)

Al^{3+}

O^{2-}

'ZUP! Al

Al^{3+}

O^{2-}

Molten Cryolite

Molten Aluminium Metal

Electrolysis is Expensive — it's all that electricity...

1) Electrolysis uses _a lot of electricity_ and that can make it pretty _expensive_.

2) Aluminium smelters usually have _their own_ hydro-electric power station _nearby_ to make the electricity as _cheap_ as possible.

3) Energy is also needed to _heat_ the electrolyte mixture to 900°C. This is expensive too.

4) The _disappearing anodes_ need frequent _replacement_. That costs money as well.

5) But in the end, aluminium now comes out as a _reasonably cheap_ and _widely-used_ metal. _A hundred years ago_ it was a very _rare_ metal, simply because it was so _hard to extract_.

Aluminium is light, strong, and corrosion-resistant

Strictly speaking you shouldn't say it's 'light', you should say it has '_low density_'. Whatever. All I know is, it's a _lot_ easier to lift and move around than iron or steel.

COMMON USES:

1) _Ladders_, _Aeroplanes_, Range Rover _body panels_ (but not the rusty tailgate!).

2) _Drink cans_, _Greenhouses_ and _window frames_.

6) Big _power cables_ used on pylons.

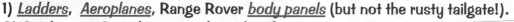

Electrolysis ain't cheap — well, there's always a charge...

Four main sections with several important points to learn for each.   Initially you might find it easiest to cover the sections one at a time and try to _recall the details_ in your head. Ultimately though you should _aim to repeat it all in one go_ with the whole page covered.

Purifying Copper by Electrolysis

1) Aluminium is a _very reactive metal_ and _has_ to be removed from its ore by _electrolysis_.

2) _Copper_ is a very _unreactive_ metal. Not only is it below carbon in the reactivity series, it's also below _hydrogen_, which means that copper doesn't even react with _water_.

3) So copper is obtained _very easily_ from its ore by _reduction_ with _carbon_.

Very pure copper is needed for electrical conductors

1) The copper produced by _reduction isn't pure enough_ for use in _electrical conductors_.

2) The _purer_ it is, the better it _conducts_. _Electrolysis_ is used to obtain _very pure copper_.

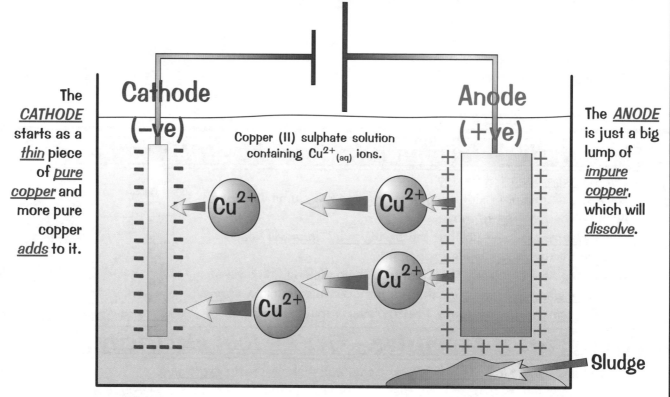

The *CATHODE* starts as a _thin_ piece of _pure copper_ and more pure copper _adds_ to it.

Cathode (–ve)

Copper (II) sulphate solution containing $Cu^{2+}_{(aq)}$ ions.

Anode (+ve)

The _ANODE_ is just a big lump of _impure copper_, which will _dissolve_.

Sludge

The *ELECTRICAL SUPPLY* acts by:

1) _Pulling electrons off_ copper atoms at the _anode_ causing them to go into solution as _Cu^{2+} ions_.

2) Then _offering electrons_ at the _cathode_ to nearby _Cu^{2+} ions_ to turn them back into _copper atoms_.

3) The _impurities_ are dropped at the _anode_ as a _sludge_, whilst _pure copper atoms_ bond to the _cathode_.

4) The electrolysis can go on for _weeks_ and the cathode is often _twenty times bigger_ at the end of it.

Pure copper is deposited on the pure cathode (–ve)

Copper dissolves from the impure anode (+ve)

Revision and electrolysis — they can both go on for weeks...

This is a pretty easy page to learn. The mini-essay method will do you proud here. Don't forget the diagram and the equations. I know it's not much fun, but think how useful all this Chemistry will be in your day-to-day life once you've learned it...

     ... hmmm, well... _learn it anyway._

Waves

Waves are different from anything else. They have various features that *only waves have*:

Amplitude, Wavelength and Frequency

Just in case you've forgotten:
1) The *AMPLITUDE* goes from the *middle* line to the *peak*, NOT from a trough to a peak.
2) The *WAVELENGTH* covers a *full cycle* of the wave, e.g. from *peak to peak*, not just from *"two bits that are sort of separated a bit"*.
3) *FREQUENCY* is how many *complete waves* there are *per second* (passing a certain point).

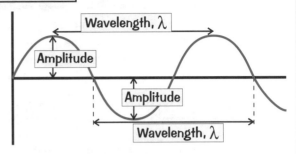

Transverse Waves Have Sideways Vibrations

Most waves are *TRANSVERSE*:

1) *Light* and all other *EM radiation*.
2) *Ripples* on water.
3) *Waves* on *strings*.
4) A *slinky spring* wiggled from side to side (or up and down).

In *TRANSVERSE WAVES* the vibrations are at 90^0 to the *direction of travel* of the wave.

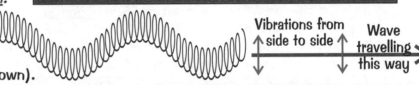

Vibrations from side to side

Wave travelling this way

Longitudinal Waves Have Vibrations Along the Same Line

The ONLY longitudinal waves are:

1) *Sound*. It travels as a longitudinal wave through solids, liquids and gases.
2) *Shock waves* e.g. seismic *P-waves*.
3) A *slinky spring* when plucked.
4) *Don't get confused* by CRO displays, which show a *transverse wave* when displaying *sound*. The real wave is *longitudinal* — the display shows a transverse wave *just so you can see what's going on*.

In *LONGITUDINAL WAVES* the vibrations are *ALONG THE SAME DIRECTION* as the wave is travelling.

One wavelength   Rarefactions

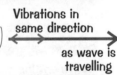

Compressions

Vibrations in same direction as wave is travelling

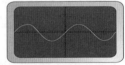

All Waves Carry Energy — Without Transferring Matter

1) *Light*, *infrared*, and *microwaves* all make things *warm up*. *X-rays* and *gamma rays* can cause *ionisation* and *damage* to cells, which also shows that they carry *energy*.
2) *Loud* sounds make things *vibrate or move*. Even the quietest sound moves your *ear drum*.
3) Waves on the sea can *toss big boats around* and can be used to generate *electricity*.

Waves Can Be REFLECTED and REFRACTED

1) They might test whether or not you realise these are *properties* of waves, so *learn them*.
2) The two words are *confusingly similar*, but you *MUST* learn the *differences* between them.
3) Light and sound are *reflected* and *refracted*, and this shows that they travel as waves.

Learn about waves — just get into the vibes, man...

This is all very basic stuff on waves. Five sections with some tasty titbits in each. *Learn* the headings, then the details. Then *cover the page* and see what you can *scribble down*. Then try again until you can remember the whole lot. It's all just *easy marks to be won... or lost*.

The Wave Equation

The speed of a wave is given by the formula $\underline{v = f\lambda}$, or
WAVE SPEED (m/s) = FREQUENCY (Hz) x WAVELENGTH (m)
This is known as the *WAVE EQUATION*, and you've gotta know it.

If you think about it, it kinda makes sense. The *frequency* is just the *number of waves* emitted *each second*, and the *wavelength* is the *length* of the wave. All the waves are *end to end*, so the total length emitted each second must be *$f\lambda$*. Since these waves must get out of the way for the next lot, they will *move this distance each second* — and how much it moves each second is simply the *speed* of the wave.

The First Rule: Try and Choose the Right Formula

1) People have *way too much difficulty* deciding which *formula* to use.
2) All too often the question starts with *"A wave is travelling..."*, and in they leap with "v = fλ".
3) To choose the *right formula* you have to look for the *THREE quantities* mentioned in the question.
4) If the question mentions *speed*, *frequency* and *wavelength* then sure, "v = fλ" is the one to use.
5) But if it has *speed*, *time* and *distance* then "s = d/t" is more the order of the day — *wouldn't you say*.

a) *Some ripples travel 55cm in 5 seconds. Find their speed in cm/s.*
   ANSWER: Speed, distance and time are mentioned in the question,
   so we must use "s=d/t":   s = d/t = 55/5 = 11cm/s.
b) *The wavelength of these waves is found to be 2.2cm. What is their frequency?*
   ANSWER: This time we have f and λ mentioned, so we use "v = fλ", and we'll need this:
   It tells us that f = v/λ = 11cm/s ÷ 2.2cm = 5Hz   (It's very cool to use cm/s with cm, s and Hz).

The Second Rule: Watch Those Units — the Little Rascals

1) The *standard (SI) units* involved with waves are: *metres*, *seconds*, *m/s* and *hertz* (Hz).

> If you want your answer in SI units, always *CONVERT INTO SI UNITS*
> (m, s, Hz, m/s) before you work anything out.

2) The trouble is waves often have *high frequencies* given in *kHz* or *MHz*, so make sure you *learn this* too:

> 1 kHz (kilohertz) = 1,000 Hz   1 MHz (megahertz) = 1,000,000 Hz

3) *Wavelengths* can also be given in *funny* units, e.g. *km* for long wave radio, or *cm* for sound.
4) There's worse still: The *speed of light* is 3×10^8 m/s = *300,000,000 m/s*. This, along with numbers like *900MHz = 900,000,000 Hz* won't fit into a lot of calculators. That leaves you *three* choices:

> 1) Enter the numbers as *standard form* (3×10^8 and 9×10^8), or...
> 2) *Cancel* three or six *noughts* off both numbers, (so long as you're *dividing* them!) or...
> 3) Do it entirely *without* a calculator (no really, I've seen it done). Your choice.

Example on Sound

Q) A sound wave travelling in a solid has a frequency of 19 kHz and a wavelength of 12cm. Find its speed.
ANSWER: We have f and λ mentioned, so we'll use "v = fλ". But we must convert the units into SI:
   So, v = f×λ = 19,000Hz × 0.12m = 2,280 m/s   — convert the units and there's no problem.

Example on EM Radiation

Q) A radio wave has a frequency of 92.2 MHz. Find its wavelength. (The speed of light is 3×10^8 m/s.)
ANSWER: We have f and λ mentioned, so we'll use "v = fλ". Radio waves travel at the speed of light, of course. Once again, we must convert the units into SI, but we'll also have to use standard form:
   λ = v/f   = 3×10^8 / 92,200,000   = 3×10^8 / 9.22×10^7 = 3.25m   (There's a few bits to get wrong).

This stuff on formulae is really painful — I mean it MHz...

Sift out the main rules on this page, then *cover it up* and *scribble them down*. Then try these:
1) A sound wave has a frequency of 2,500Hz and a wavelength of 13.2cm. Find its speed.
2) The radio waves for Radio 4 have a wavelength of 1.5 km. Find their frequency.

Total Internal Reflection

Total internal reflection only happens when *light* is *coming out* of something *dense* like *glass* or *water* or *perspex*. If the *angle* is *shallow enough* the ray *won't come out at all*, but it *reflects* back into the glass (or whatever). This is called *total internal reflection* because __ALL__ of the light *reflects back in*.

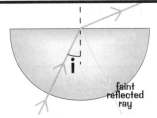 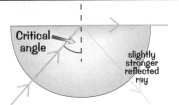 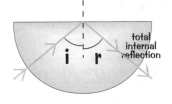

Angle of Incidence LESS than the Critical Angle — Most of the light *passes through* into the air but a *little* bit of it is *internally reflected*.

Angle of Incidence EQUAL TO the Critical Angle — The emerging ray comes out *along the surface*. There's quite a bit of *internal reflection*.

Angle of Incidence GREATER than the Critical Angle — *No light comes out*. It's *all* internally reflected, i.e. *total internal reflection*.

The *Critical Angle* for *glass* is about 42°. This is *very handy* because it means *45° angles* can be used to get *total internal reflection* as in the *prisms* in the *binoculars* and *periscope*:

Binoculars

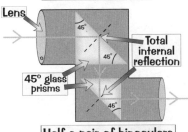

Half a pair of binoculars

Binoculars and the *periscope* use prisms because they give slightly *better reflection* than a *mirror* would, and they're also *easier* to hold accurately *in place*. Learn the exact *positioning* of the prisms. They could ask you to *complete* a diagram of a binocular or periscope and unless you've *practised* beforehand you'll find it *pretty tricky* to draw the prisms in *properly*.
Total Internal Reflection is used in *binoculars* and *periscopes*. Both use *45° prisms*.

Periscope

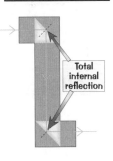

Optical Fibres — Communications and Endoscopes

1) *Optical fibres* can carry *information* over *long distances* by repeated *total internal reflections*.
2) Optical communications have several *advantages* over *electrical signals* in wires:
   a) the signal doesn't need *boosting* as often.
   b) a cable of the *same diameter* can carry a lot *more information*.
   c) the signals cannot be *tapped into*, or suffer *interference* from electrical sources.
3) Normally no light whatever would be lost at each reflection. However some light *is lost* due to *imperfections* in the surface, so it still needs *boosting* every *few km*. The fibre must be *narrow enough* to keep the angles *above* the critical angle, as shown, and the fibre mustn't be bent *too sharply* anywhere.

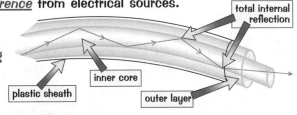

Endoscopes Are Used to Look Inside People

This is a *narrow bunch* of *optical fibres* with a *lens system* at each end. Another bunch of optical fibres carries light down *inside* to see with. The image is displayed as a *full colour moving image* on a **TV** screen. Real impressive stuff. This means they can do operations *without* cutting big holes in people. This was never possible before optical fibres.

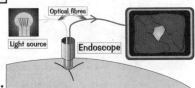

Total internal reflection — sounds like a government inquiry...

First and foremost make sure you can *scribble all the diagrams* down with all the details. Then *scribble a mini-essay* for each topic, jotting down everything you can remember. Then check back and see what you *missed*. Then *learn the stuff you forgot* and *try again*. Ahh... such fun.

Diffraction

This word sounds a lot more technical than it really is.

Diffraction Is Just the "Spreading Out" of Waves

All waves tend to *spread out* at the *edges* when they pass through a *gap* or *past an object*. Instead of saying that the wave *"spreads out"* or *"bends"* round a corner, you should say that it *DIFFRACTS* around the corner. It's as easy as that. That's all diffraction means.

A Wave Spreads More if It Passes Through a Narrow Gap

The *ripple tank* shows this effect quite nicely. The same effect applies to *light* and *sound* too.

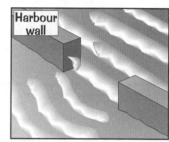

Harbour wall

1) A *"narrow"* gap is one which is about the *same size* as the *wavelength* or *less*.
2) Obviously then, the question of whether a gap is *"narrow"* or not depends on the *wave* in question. What may be a *narrow* gap for a *water* wave will be a *huge* gap for a *light* wave.
3) It should be obvious then, that the *longer* the wavelength of a wave, *the more it will diffract*.

Sounds Always Diffract Quite a Lot, Because λ is Quite Big

1) Most sounds have wavelengths *in air* of around *0.1m*, which is quite long.
2) This means they *spread out round corners* so you can still *hear* people even when you can't *see* them directly (the sound usually *reflects* off walls too which also helps).
3) *Higher frequency sounds* will have *shorter wavelengths* and so they won't diffract as much, which is why things sound more *"muffled"* when you hear them from round corners.

Long Wavelength Radio Waves Diffract Easily over Hills and into Buildings:

Shorter wavelength TV and FM radio do not diffract very much

Long wavelength radio waves diffract

These houses will get reception of long wave radio, but not TV or FM radio

Visible Light on the Other Hand...

has a *very short wavelength*, and it'll only diffract with a *very narrow slit*:

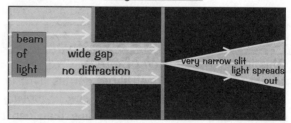

beam of light

wide gap no diffraction

very narrow slit light spreads out

This spreading or *diffraction* of light (and radio waves) is *strong evidence* for the *wave nature of light*.

Diffraction — it can drive you round the bend...

People usually don't know much about diffraction, mainly because there are so few lab demos you can do to show it, and there's also very little to say about it — about one page's worth, in fact. The thing is though, if you just *learn this page properly*, then you'll *know all you need to*.

Seismic Waves

Seismic Waves Reveal the Earth's Structure

1) *Seismic waves* are caused by *earthquakes*. They're pretty handy for telling us what the Earth's like inside. Without them, we'd only know about the first *10km* or so — that's how far we can *drill*.
2) Measurements of the waves reveal that the Earth has a *core*, which is divided into an *inner core* (pretty *solid)* and an *outer core* (*liquid*).
3) Outside the core you've got the *mantle*, which is basically *pretty solid*, though it does *flow a bit* under the enormous *pressures*.
4) The final bit is the *crust*, which ranges in thickness from about 10km under the oceans to about 80km under the highest mountains. Pretty *flimsy* really — that's all there is between us and the *fiery depths*.

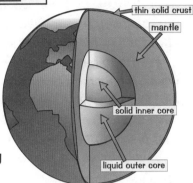

S-Waves and P-Waves Take Different Paths

P-Waves Are Longitudinal

P-Waves travel through both *solids and liquids*. They travel *faster* than *S-waves*.

No P-waves reach here

P-waves pass through core and are detected here

S-Waves Are Transverse

S-Waves will *only* travel through *solids*. They're *slower* than *P-waves*.

No S waves reach here, they can't pass through the core

Seismographs Tells Us What's Down There

1) About *halfway* through the Earth, there's an abrupt *change in direction* of both types of wave. This indicates that there's a sudden *increase in density* at that point — the *CORE*.
2) The fact that S-waves are *not* detected in the *shadow* of this core tells us that it's very *liquid*.
3) It's also found that *P-waves* travel *slightly faster* through the *middle* of the core, which strongly suggests that there's a *solid inner core*.
4) Note that *S-waves* do travel through the *mantle*, which suggests that it's kinda *solid*, though I always thought it was made of *molten lava* which looks pretty *liquidy* to me when it comes *sploshing* out of volcanoes. Still there you go, just another one of life's little conundrums, I guess.

The Paths Curve Due to Increasing Density (Causing Refraction)

1) Both *S-waves* and *P-waves* travel *faster* in *more dense* material.
2) The *curvature* of their paths is due to the *increasing density* of the *mantle* and *core* with depth.
3) When the density changes *suddenly*, the waves change direction *abruptly*, as shown above.
4) The paths *curve* because the density of both the mantle and the core *increases steadily* with increasing depth. The waves *gradually change direction* because their speed is *gradually changing*, due to gradual changes in the *density* of the medium. This is *refraction*, of course.

Seismic waves — they reveal the terrible trembling truth...

The last page on waves. Hoorah. Once again there are four main sections to learn. *Learn* the headings first, then try *scribbling down* all the details for each heading, including the diagrams. Remember that S-waves are tran*S*ver*S*e — so P-waves must be the longitudinal ones.

Revision Summary for Module Nine

The Universe is completely mind-blowing in its own right. But surely the most mind-blowing thing of all is the very fact that we are actually here, sitting and contemplating the truly outrageous improbability of our own existence. If your mind isn't blowing, then it hasn't sunk in yet. Think about it. 15 billion years ago there was a huge explosion, but there was no need for the whole chain of events to happen that allowed (or caused?) intelligent life to evolve and develop to the point where it became conscious of its own existence, not to mention the very disturbing unlikelihood of it all. But we have. We're here. Maaaan — is that freaky or what? The Universe could so easily have existed without conscious life ever evolving. Or come to that, the Universe needn't exist at all. Just black nothingness. So why does it exist? And why are we here?

And why do we have to do so much revision? Who knows — but stop dreaming and get on with it.

1) What is the main theory of the origin of the Universe? Give brief details of the theory.
2) Describe an important piece of evidence for this theory.
3) Approximately how long ago did the Universe begin?
4) Describe the first stages of a star's formation. Where does the initial energy come from?
5) What process eventually starts inside the star to make it produce so much heat and light?
6) What are the final two stages of a small star's life?
7) What gases did the early atmosphere consist of? Where did these gases come from?
8) What was the main thing which caused phase two of the atmosphere's evolution?
9) Which gases became much less common and which one increased?
10) Which gas allowed phase three to take place?
11) What are the percentages of gases in today's atmosphere?
12) What are the three types of rock? Draw a full diagram of the rock cycle.
13) What are found in sedimentary rocks but are not found in any other type of rock?
14) Draw a diagram to show how metamorphic rocks are formed. What does the name mean?
15) What are the two main metamorphic rocks? Describe their appearance and give a use for each.
16) How are igneous rocks formed? What are the two types? Give an example of each.
17) What is the difference in the way that they formed and in their structure and appearance?
18) Draw a diagram of the internal structure of the Earth, with labels.
19) Where is the San Andreas fault? What are the tectonic plates doing along this fault line?
20) What happens when an oceanic plate collides with a continental plate? Draw a diagram.
21) What are rocks, ores and minerals? Name a metal found as a metal rather than a compound?
22) Draw a diagram of a blast furnace. What are the three raw materials used in it?
23) Write down the equations for how iron is obtained from its ore in the blast furnace.
24) How is aluminium extracted from its ore? Give four operational details and draw a diagram.
25) Give a reason why this process is so expensive.
26) How is copper extracted from its ore? How is it then purified, and why does it need to be?
27) Give three uses each for iron (or steel) and aluminium.
28) Sketch a transverse wave. Give a definition for it. Give four examples of transverse waves.
29) Sketch a longitudinal wave. Give a definition for it. Give two examples of longitudinal waves.
30) Give three examples of waves carrying energy.
31) What are the two formulae involved with waves? How do you decide which one to use?
32) What are the standard units for: a) wavelength b) frequency c) velocity d) time?
33) Sketch the three diagrams to illustrate total internal reflection and the critical angle.
34) Sketch two applications of total internal reflection that use 45° prisms, and explain them.
35) Give details of the two main uses of optical fibres. How do optical fibres work?
36) What is diffraction? Sketch the diffraction of a) water waves b) sound waves c) light.
37) Describe the Earth's inner structure. What do seismographs tell us about the structure of the Earth?
38) What causes seismic waves? Sketch diagrams showing the paths of both types, and explain.

Index

Index